REFLECTION ON LIFE IN BUFFALO NY (1932–92)

REFLECTION ON LIFE IN BUFFALO NY (1932–92)

A personal journal by
THOMAS J MURPHY

iUniverse, Inc.
New York Lincoln Shanghai

REFLECTION ON LIFE IN BUFFALO NY (1932–92)

iUniverse books may be ordered through booksellers or by contacting:

iUniverse
2021 Pine Lake Road, Suite 100
Lincoln, NE 68512
www.iuniverse.com
1-800-Authors (1-800-288-4677)

ISBN-13: 978-0-595-40858-0 (pbk)
ISBN-13: 978-0-595-85222-2 (ebk)
ISBN-10: 0-595-40858-3 (pbk)
ISBN-10: 0-595-85222-X (ebk)

Printed in the United States of America

Contents

PREFACE

"Know your place in the world and judge yourself fairly, not according to the romantic ideals of your youth, nor according to the ideals of your peers, but according to yourself."

—Richard F Feynman
Scientist/Humanist/Scholar

John McGahern, an Irish writer, described his talent, and his tasks, in the following words, "Each of us has a private world, and the only difference between the reader and the writer is that the writer has the ability to describe and dramatize that private world. As a writer, I write to see. If I knew how it would end, I wouldn't write. It's a process of discovery."

When I began writing my memoirs it was more a mental exercise than anything else. I went back to my earliest memories and then advanced year by year, jotting down recalled observations and sometimes incidents, as I remembered them. I eventually titled this first manuscript, *"Growing Up and Growing Old in Buffalo NY: A Very Personal Memoir"*.

I could never attest to the accuracy of my writing, only to it's honesty. But then there came several occasions when I had finished writing about a thought, or an emotion, from the distant past, and I would realize that I had never expressed that memory verbally or in writing before. The act of writing had become a "process of discovery" and the experience was exhilarating, not because it was a challenge, or even an opportunity to explain or atone, but because I had become anxious to relive, to experience anew, and to reexamine long forgotten feelings and sensations.

As I proceeded in my new avocation I took great care to only express my feelings and emotions, without apology and without undue analysis. My primary audience continued to be "myself", but I readily acknowledged that this was also my best, and probably last, opportunity to reveal myself to my family and 'loved ones'. Therefore, I strove to eliminate self-aggrandizement and self-abasement references from the text. I was careful never to represent another's thoughts, motives, or emotions There was never any intention or desire that *"Growing Up and Growing Old in Buffalo NY"*, which is a very personal memoir, become a public document.

A limited number of copies of the finished manuscript were self-published and distributed to my family members, and to a few close friends. The immediate response was most gratifying. Friends called to thank me for the book, to discuss and to critique or question, or to ask that I elaborate on passages that they found interesting. Mostly they expressed appreciation for the effort that is required to complete such a project. In the song *"Arianne"* there is a line "happy as the writer who discovers he's been read" that amply described my feeling. I gained considerable warmth and satisfaction from the knowledge that several of those who had liked me previously, continued to like me, after they had shared my most private thoughts. But as the months went by, the euphoria faded. The response I received from family members was a collective yawn. When I asked one of my daughters for her reaction to the book she replied, "I read it and put it on my bookshelf". The same question posed to a son drew the response "I haven't had a chance to read it!" and another daughter replied "I didn't understand a word of it!" Another 'loved one' described the effort as "a slight fantasy". I immediately stopped soliciting "reviews". I was puzzled and disappointed. While I hadn't expected that my written thoughts would erase all aches of past indignities and embarrassments, I had hoped that my children would excuse my lack of contrition, and that we would be able to proceed into a renewed relationship, free of doubts or thoughts of retribution, regret or recrimination.

Then after several more months of silence, my daughter Linda, who has always been my muse, my 'scold', and 'my favorite', found an occasion to critique my memoir. She wrote, "I was hurt that there were no stories or details of fun times as a family. We (children) certainly did not come off as being an important part of you."

I was stunned! I had been afraid that what I had written had given offense to some of my 'loved ones'. Now I found that some of my children were offended because I didn't write a different type of memoir. However, I welcomed the opportunity to reopen our dialogue and to rethink my purposes for writing.

My first reaction to Linda's comment was to immediately acknowledge that "family life" had certainly been secondary to my role as "breadwinner". I tried to explain that this 'attitude' should not be interpreted as a lack of my love, affection, or respect for any family member. I recoiled at the realization that some of my children had narcissistically sought evidence of my affection for them in my memoirs. It seemed to me that they had failed to explore, or to grasp, the introspective notions that constituted the bulk of the manuscript.

I reflected at some length as to whether an intrapersonal journal had been the appropriate vehicle for expressing my appreciation and love for those who had enriched my life. I came to the conclusion that it had.. Any other approach would be reproachfully fanciful. Many of the "…that Christmas we had the biggest tree I ever saw!" books were written from a child's perspective. "A Tree Grows in Brooklyn", "Angela's Ashes" and "Life with Father" come readily to mind. Yet I had opened my memoirs with the sentence, "My memories of childhood are neither bleak or carefree". My youthful relationship with my parents, and younger sister, could best be described as "chary", never warm and cuddly. Hardly 'great novel' stuff!

My teen-age years were neither "Catcher in the Rye", "Leave It To Beaver", nor "Mean Streets". I hadn't been exposed to sexual or physical abuse. I hadn't been confronted by pedophiles, sexual deviates or drug pushers. My parents, who were not particularly loving, were never abusive to me, of themselves or to each other, nor were they alcoholics or dysphorics.

That left me with only "Father of the Bride" or "Father Knows Best" alternative narrations. I have many beautiful memories of warm, witty and loving family occasions, which will remain with me and enrich my spirit, for as long as I live. I remember dozens, maybe hundreds, of occasions when one or more of our children displayed a precociousness, an endearing quality, or performed an act of love or charity. I remember my children's awards and accomplishments. There were victories and defeats on athletic fields, in classrooms, in courtrooms, and in homes and apartments far from other's eyes. Each child had love affairs, and I presume that a few were disappointed in love affairs.

But what if I were to write that I was proud of the fact that five of our children had achieved "straight A's' while in the fifth grade of school. What then should I write, if anything, about the scholastic records of the remaining three children?

If I wrote a glowing review of a marriage ceremony, "attended only by two loving families, and a few very close friends, brimming with affection and respect for the wedded couple", am I compelled then to similarly comment on each family wedding? And what if another family member remembered this same occasion as, "two antagonistic families, glaring at each other from across the aisle, blaming the 'other side' for forcing a scandalous union"?

Can praise for "a happy marriage, blessed with beautiful, intelligent and darling grandchildren", foster resentment, or despair, from children engaged in a loving, but childless marriage, or from divorced or single siblings?

I've decided that it is in my best interest that I continue to write, but I'll also continue to retain "happy family times" in my memory bank, along with any resentment that I might hold because of real or imagined 'slights'. As I edit and expand on my recollections I'll remember that representations of how others performed, felt or reacted at past, shared events are often twisted or misunderstood, and I will leave these recollections to others. We can only 'know' what's in our own hearts! And sometimes, even what we really 'know' is better if it isn't shared! 'Airing dirty laundry' is never a good idea!

So on the following pages you'll not find 'happy' recollections of family picnics, or mementos of days spent at the beach, or samples of 'wit and wisdom' from deceased relatives or school chums. Instead, I'll try to examine a little more closely the people that I've met, the jobs that interested me, and the opinions that I've held, in order to ascertain whether I've gathered any 'wheat along with the chaff'. I'll try to follow Mr McGahern's advice and only relate what 'I' did and felt at different times and in different places. I'll report what 'I' think about current and past conditions and maybe I can explain and describe my 'private world' and those factors that made 'me' the man that I've become.

1

PRE-TEEN YEARS

*"The unrecorded past is none other than our old friend, the tree in
the primeval forest which fell without being heard."*

—Barbara Tuchman, author and historian

My memories of childhood are neither bleak nor carefree. I was born in 1932.
Thus, my first ten years of life were filled with the certainties that FDR was
always going to be U.S. President, Pius XII was the eternal Catholic Pope (and
quite likely would be named a saint), Joe Louis was the only heavyweight champion of the world, and one dollar was a rare and precious commodity,—and
nothing much was ever going to change.

So many biographies today spell out tales of neglect or abuse of youngsters. I was
never neglected nor abused. My mother, Catherine (Kay) Murphy, often worked
full time as a stenographer at a local construction supply company during the
Depression and early days of World War II, leaving my sister and me in care of
teen-aged babysitters, but I never recall any emergencies or bad behavior arising
from this situation.

My father, Thomas J Murphy Sr, was a likeable, fun loving Irishman. In his
younger and middle years he was often mistaken for Fred McMurray, the movie
actor. However, Dad's character most resembled that of Sgt. Ernie Bilko, televi-
son character, who loved poker, gambling, and was always attempting to gain the
upper hand on the rest of the civilized world. Dad drank, I saw him intoxicated
on several occasions,—but he was a garrulous, not a quarrelsome drinker,—there
was no problem of alcoholism. All night poker games were no rarity in the Murphy household, but I was never aware of any financial damage from gambling
losses.

My first clear recollections are of our family living at 372 West Avenue and my attending classes at Holy Angels Parochial School, and singing in the Boy's Choir while attending Mass at Holy Angels Church, which was located on Porter Avenue, only one-half block from my residence. Until 1942, my father was employed as 'custodian' at Grover Cleveland High School, which was within easy walking distance of our home at York and Jersey Streets. The Porter-Best bus ran on Porter Avenue and traversed the City in an East-West direction. The Grant Street bus went by our front door, and provided easy access to both Downtown Buffalo and the Grant-Ferry neighborhood shopping district.

The neighborhood, Buffalo's West Side, with giant chestnut trees lining every curbside, displayed a multi-national cultural hue. French-speaking Grey Nuns of the Sacred Heart had established D'Youville College (for girls) on Porter Avenue, across from Prospect Park, and these nuns also taught at Holy Angels Parochial School. The Oblate Fathers, (founded in France), were the clerics at Holy Angels Church and had established a seminary at the corner of West Avenue and Porter Avenue. Horse drawn (ice and rags) wagons, electric (milk) carts and motorized 'kiddie' rides, regularly plied their trade on the neighborhood streets., Don Kramer (German) operated the corner delicatessen at Porter and Plymouth Street, Bill Provost (French) owned the local grocery and butcher shop on Plymouth Ave. and Fourteenth Street, Donahue's Drug Store was at Normal Ave at Jersey Street, and Italian fruit and vegetable stands, bakeries, meat markets, restaurants, and specialty shops lined both sides of Connecticut Street between West Ave. and York Street. Famed park designer, Frederick Law Olmstead, had designed Porter Avenue as a broad vista between Prospect Park and Symphony Circle, where Richmond Avenue began. Porter Avenue was lined by gracious homes, then owned and occupied by doctors, politicians, and prominent business men. Kleinhans Music Hall, with it's reflection pool, situated at Symphony Circle, provided an exclamation mark to the idyllic scene.

Our neighbors on West Avenue, were Mr & Mrs Salmon, and Mrs Slater. Mr Salmon was retired from Hanna Furnace Corp. and Mrs Slater, a tiny wizened lady, was either a widow or a spinster. Both gave me regular, part-time work, which provided me with nickles and dimes,—my own spending money! My classmates at Holy Angles were Billy O'Connor, Davie O'Brien, John Carroll, Jack Kehoe, Robert Comforto, Leonard Sapienza, Frank Marchiello, Carl D'Auria, Barbara Christina and Dick Hoffman. I'll never understand how Hoffman, a German, ever insinuated himself into this bunch of Italians and Irish!

I was not deprived,—I never remember being hungry, nor feeling needier than my friends and classmates,—except that Billy Provost, whose father owned a grocery store, always seemed to have candy or soda pop at his disposal.. The Kehoes, who lived across the street, vacationed for three weeks each summer, with the whole family picking strawberries! And they were paid for doing it! Now I realize that the entire Kehoe family was employed as "day labor", each doing back-aching 'picking' in order to earn a few cents for each hour worked. But at that time, how I envied them their beautiful tans and the hours they spent frolicking through the sunny, delicious fields.

Spacious Front Park, with several baseball diamonds; Prospect Park, manicured and serene; Holy Angels playground, with two handball courts; and sedate Symphony Circle, were only a few minutes from our homes, but we preferred to play our 'kick-the-can', 'mumbly peg', 'Nip' and impromptu ball games, in Cobb Alley, a service lane that ran between Porter Avenue and Jersey Street, behind West Avenue homes.

While I've stated that my childhood was not bleak,—it is hard to call to mind happy memories. Until the age of ten, sports was a difficult and sometimes painful undertaking. Playing baseball meant catching a 'hard' ball, either bare handed, or with a mitt with little, if any, padding. Only a catcher's mitt had a pocket and only a first baseman's glove had a catchable webbing. "Catch the ball with two hands" was an admonishment necessitated by the fact that a thrown or batted baseball could not be retained in the pocket of a regular fielder's glove. Hitting a hardball almost always resulted in stinging hands, since most baseball bats that we had were cracked. As a youngster, I was gangling and slow afoot. Racing, or running from a fight or a bully, was a hopeless endeavor. Football invariably resulted in torn clothing as a result of tackling, or stumbles, on hard, stony ground. It seems that we could never find, or were not permitted to play on grassy areas. The only sport that seemed enjoyable was handball, played with a rubber ball (not hard) that was slightly larger than a handball, but smaller than a baseball.

Most of the games that we played were simple, and unorganized. Toys were sometimes homemade and almost always 'bandaged' or in need of repair. The game,'Nip', was played with a round stick, 12" to 18" long, which was used to strike and drive a 3" stick, which had been whittled to a point at both ends, towards a telephone pole or other 'goal'. I suppose this game was our precursor to the game of 'golf'. We made our own 'scooters' out of a 3' plank, an orange crate, and a broken roller skate. Baseballs, and baseball bats, were invariably mended with electrical tape to prevent unraveling, or to keep them in one piece. We could fashion a non-lethal, but effective version of a 'zip' gun, by strategically combining a 16" piece of 2"X4", with a half of clothespin, a nail, and a tire inner tube, that had been sliced into 1' bands. Ammunition for these weapons was more inner-tube bands, knotted in the center to increase velocity when 'fired'. I also possessed the more conventional toys,-tops, yo-yos, lead soldiers, a toy helmet and cap pistols. Every boy I knew collected comic books (which were often traded) and 'war cards', which were either traded or gambled in a game where they were pitched against a wall, with the one closest to the wall winning the other pitched cards.

Each Saturday afternoon, summer or winter—come rain or come shine,—was spent in a neighborhood movie house. Two theaters, The Circle and The Senate were within easy walking distance of my home. A third neighborhood 'show', The Victoria, was located on Grant Street but could be easily reached by taking the Grant Street bus for a fare of only 3 cents. At each theater the price of admission for a Saturday matinee was one nickle. The normal program was ten cartoons, three cowboy movies (Johnny Mack Brown, Tim Holt, Gene Autry, etc), and one serial (Captain Marvel, Dick Tracy, etc). The Circle Theater also threw in a free comic book for each patron. For the most part, weekday late afternoons were spent listening to the radio. "Jack Armstrong" (The All-American Boy), "I Love a Mystery", and "Stella Dallas" were my particular favorites. It was also about this time that I became a New York Yankee baseball fan, and occasionally I could pick up a radio broadcast of one of the Yankee's day games.

Even though these earliest years were spent in the depths of the Great Depression, I never lacked for employment, or for spending money. Beginning at age eight, Mr. and Mrs. Salmon, who lived next door, hired me to fill their furnace hopper with 14 buckets of coal each night at 5 PM. and fetch the evening paper from Kramer's Delicatessen (½ block away). My pay was 10 cents weekly. During the summer months, the Salmon's would occasionally ask me to weed their backyard, (my pay was 10 cents for a bushel of weeds), and Mrs. Slater paid me 10 cents each Saturday morning to mow her tiny front lawn, repair her leaking garden hose, and hose down the concrete floor of her rear garage. In no way was this employment meant to be, nor interpreted by me as demeaning. Rather, I know now, and I think that I knew then, that our neighbors had found a gracious and dignified means of sharing their larder. For my part, I certainly didn't mind the work and the spending money was most welcome.

There is much discussion today about physical abuse of children by Roman Catholic clergy and religious personnel. In my first ten years, the only disciplinary action inflicted upon me was when my first grade teacher, Sister Mary Jane, required that I sit on the floor, under her desk, when I misbehaved. She continued this practice until the day that the Pastor of the Parish, Father Rivers, visited the classroom and seemed shocked when I stuck my head from beneath the teacher's desk.—I don't recall ever having to suffer solitary confinement again.

I recall attending a few birthday parties for friends and classmates while living on Buffalo's West Side,—I was introduced to cream cheese and jelly sandwiches at Barbara Christina's party,—but I never remember celebrating my birthday in any way.

My Dad was always looking for an opportunity to make a few extra dollars. He served as a 'marshall' at high school football games on Saturday afternoons at All-High stadium. He refereed amateur hockey games in Memorial Auditorium on Sunday afternoons. And he taught 'badminton' to adults at 'night school'. This extracurricular activity meant that Dad wasn't at home much of the time, and seldom were my parents at home together. My mother, my sister Patricia, and I spent most Sunday afternoons, which was my mother's only day off from work, at my grandmother "Ma" Griffins house, on South Park Avenue, in Buffalo's Old First Ward. Occasionally, the three of us would attend a matinee at a downtown movie house, or we would ride the trolley out to Cazenovia Park to watch Muny League baseball being played. But seldom did we spend weekends together as a family unit.

In 1942, my father was 37 years old, no longer eligible to be drafted into the Armed Forces, but anxious that he not be considered a draft dodger, or 4F. He applied for and received an appointment as an inspector in the US Border Patrol. He was immediately sent to El Paso TX for three months training. Upon completion of training he was assigned to duty at the US Navy Air Station in Pensacola FL, where there weren't any provisions for domiciling families of civilian personnel. Like thousands of others, our family life had been abruptly altered by wartime service. My mother continued to work at Beals, but more and more each day, she began to view me as 'the man of the house', much as she had always regarded her brother "Jimmy", who continued to 'reign supreme' at my grandmother's home. She also increasingly looked to me for companionship, shared confidences with me, and even sought my guidance. Mom was a comely woman, (to my eyes she most resembled Theresa Wright, the movie actress), but she didn't easily make friends. She never learned to drive a car and this further isolated her from old friends and family. I believe that the World War II years were particularly lonely for her, although I never heard her admit to that.

Eventually, we received the news that my father had once again been reassigned, this time to West Palm Beach FL. Happily, the entire family was able to accompany him this time and we were to report to the new post in late January 1943. Thus began six months spent in idyllic, exotic, subtropical, wartime West Palm Beach Fl. Here I caught my first, and last fish, saw rattlesnakes, pelicans, cardinals and bluejays, played shuffleboard, and frolicked among the crashing waves of the Atlantic Ocean.

It was also where I first observed unusual treatment of people because of race. Of course, Florida was still segregated at that time, but to a young boy there seemed nothing wrong with separate water fountains, restrooms, and restaurants,—or even the requirement that Negroes ride in the back of the bus. But, I witnessed on several occasions Negro women, boarding a bus at the front door, climbing two steps, depositing their fare in the fare box, exiting the bus to reenter by the rear door and having the bus driver pull off without opening the rear door. I don't recall anyone ever protesting.

Shortly after our arrival in Florida, my mother, my sister, and I rode a bus for our first visit to downtown West Palm Beach. When we arrived in the small business district and alit from the vehicle, we were truly sightseers, and had no idea where to go, or what to see. We chose to walk to the neighborhood to the right of the main drag (a bus route). One block from where we had stepped off the bus, we found ourselves in the Negro quarters. The street was unpaved and the sidewalks were wooden. We were terrified! And as we proceeded along the sidewalk, Negro pedestrians got off the sidewalk to let us pass. One didn't have to be a Rhode's scholar or to be of voting age to realize that there was great injustice in the "Old South."

On another occasion, I was alone in downtown West Palm Beach. Shoeshine stands were quite commonplace during those times and I decided that I would get my shoes shined.. I approached the Negro attendant and said "Can I get my shoes shined, boy?". He nodded and gestured for me to climb onto the elevated seat and footrest. As he was applying the first layer of polish, without raising his head or eyes, he asked "How old are you?". "Twelve," I lied, thinking that I might have breeched some city ordinance or standard. He looked up then, our eyes met and this gray-haired man said to me, "Do I look like a boy to you?". "No, you don't sir." I answered apologetically, and I had learned a lesson in civility, and dignity, and courage which I have never forgotten.

I don't mean to imply that the six months we lived in Florida were spent in a hostile or unpleasant environment, for that certainly was not the case. I was not aware of any racial tension. Though it was wartime, our only acknowledgment of this fact was a perpetual 'brownout' at night (U-boats were offshore) and the fact that nuns in school asked us to pray for the crews of aircraft overhead because they were probably heading overseas. Otherwise, life was quite normal. My sister and I attended the only parochial school in West Palm Beach (St Ann's). I was one of the tallest members of my class and had to fight (wrestle) other large boys to demonstrate that I wouldn't be bullied. I was given the singing lead in the school's St Patrick's Day Play and sang solos "Rose of Tralee" and "I'll take you home again Kathleen." Noon times were spent "matching pennies" and more than once Pat and I were forced to walk home from school because I had lost our carfare gambling with classmates.

I don't recall having any 'good' friends among my Florida classmates. And, I don't think that we had any neighbors (and certainly no other children) living anywhere in proximity to our home at 311 31st Street. As in Buffalo, Mom, Pat and I would often spend Sunday at a movie theater. Occasionally, we would cross the causeway to attend the movie in Palm Beach. Leaving West Palm Beach and entering Palm Beach was akin to Dorothy and Toto arriving in Oz! The palms in Palm Beach were all Hawaiian Royal. Retail establishments, whether soda shoppes, clothing stores, or restaurants could only be described as 'chic'. As far as I can tell, we were the only three people to visit Palm Beach during WWII and not meet or cavort with the clan of Joseph Kennedy!

In contrast with bustling, crowded Buffalo, WWII West Palm Beach seemed to be a small, sleepy Southern town, whose main industry was Morrison Field, an Army Air Force base which ferried military personnel and supplies to North Africa. The city had been gridded, but many of the residentially zoned blocks were simply overgrown, jungle like areas, with no sidewalks or utility lines, surrounded by right of ways (sometimes unpaved). All of the sidewalks were strewn with coconuts. During the six months that we had resided in Florida the weather had been ideal, (we hadn't experienced summertime heat), the community had been hospitable, we lived in a comfortable home, and we were looking forward to spending several more years in our new environs. We then received word that My Dad had been reassigned again! We were returning to Buffalo NY.

Upon our return to Buffalo, my parents rented a lower flat at 229 Blaine Avenue, a quiet, pleasant residential neighborhood. Pat and I were enrolled at St Vincent's Parochial School. I don't recall having any close friends either among my classmates or neighbors during this period.

I have memories of what seemed to be a perpetual game of Monopoly being played on our front porch, and another game, similar to a combination tag and hide and seek, played most evenings after dinner in the backyards and alleyways along Blaine Avenue. Formal sports were confined to touch football (played by mostly high school students) both on the quiet residential street and occasionally in the green, treed area between Humboldt Pkwy, (now part of the Kensington Expressway). My football position was primarily pass rusher or blocker and didn't contribute much to my appreciation of football as a sport or as a worthwhile endeavor.

Once we returned to Buffalo, my quest for gainful employment resumed. During the first weeks that we lived on Blaine Avenue, I visited every grocery, delicatessen and drugstore within a three-block radius. Everywhere I went, it seemed that I was too young for employment even though I had a series of fake Baptismal certificates showing that I was born in 1931, 1929, and 1928. Actually, I had turned 11 years old shortly after we moved onto Blaine Avenue. I remember one grocer, after I presented evidence that I was 12 years old, telling me that he would only hire me if I could lift a full case of bottled beer, and when I easily hoisted the crate, the owner told me that I had to be 16 to work where alcoholic beverages were sold.

Failing to find anyone willing to pay for my labor, I eventually hit upon the idea that I could raise chickens in the top (second) floor of the garage behind our home. Despite the fact that a nearby grocer had told me that he would buy all the eggs that I could supply, my father immediately quashed what could have become Buffalo's first urban hennery.

Schooling at St. Vincent is but a dim memory. My teacher, a nun, discovered that I had the unusual ability to reproduce with a pencil, whatever I saw with my eyes. She assigned me to copy and enlarge a number of Christmas card scenes and to transcribe these images onto the classroom blackboard, using colored chalk. I didn't mind at all, for it was a very pleasant way to spend the school day. I vaguely remember that when another nun questioned whether drawing on the blackboard was the most productive use of my time, my teacher responded that I already knew the assigned text material and that I had received the art assignment as a reward.

At this time, my father was employed by the US Border Patrol and assigned to check for expatriates at both the Peace Bridge and at the foot of Ferry Street, where an auto ferry traversed the Niagara River between Buffalo and Fort Erie, Ontario. My mother had returned to the stenographer's position at Beals, McCarthy and Rogers, at least on a part-time basis. Poker games, lasting far into the night, were still held on a regular and frequent basis in our home, and I often stood, fascinated by watching the hands being played, far past my normal bed-time.

Then one day I was told that the landlord of the property wanted to move back into their home, and that my father had made a down payment on a home for us, without my mother's knowledge, on Coe Place in Buffalo. Coe Place was a narrow street, barely wide enough for two vehicles, that extended approximately 150 yards between Main Street and Ellicott Street. The homes on the street were old, wood framed, multistoried buildings. There were neither front nor side yards. A few of the houses had tiny backyards and 35 Coe Place, our home, had the only ancillary structure on the street. It was little more than a shed, too small to be a garage and so dilapidated that I don't recall anything ever being stored in it. It turned out that a previous owner had used the shed as a place to manufacture bleaches and washing solutions. The backyard also contained two cherry trees but the small confines of the yard would permit nothing else, even grass, to grow.

Our residence was in some respects an amazing structure. The house was extremely narrow and the first floor where we lived consisted of a tiny living room (8'X10'), a dining room (10'X12'), a small bedroom (Dad's), a medium sized bedroom (Mom and Pat in a double bed and me in a single bed), together with a small kitchen and a minute bathroom.

The second floor was where the amazement occurred. It was divided into two apartments, with tenants sharing one tiny bathroom. In the front was a one room apartment, occupied for as long as I lived there, by an elderly spinster, with her radio and hotplate. The rear, one bedroom apartment, had a series of tenants, only two of whom I recall—one was my cousin, Eddie Ruh and his bride, who lived in the apartment the first year of their marriage. Then there was a single mother, along with her beautiful teenaged daughter (five years my elder). Any other tenants are only a blur and I have no idea what rents were collected, or how much income my parents derived from these arrangements. After about two years, my bed was moved into the third floor attic and I slept there during my high school years.

Thus, in January 1944, Pat and I entered our fourth elementary school in two years, Our Lady of Lourdes. Class sizes were small and my sixth grade classmates and I shared classroom space with fifth grade students, all under the tutelage of Sister Christina. Here is where I would strike up my first lifelong friendships.

I was about to describe Our Lady of Lourdes as a 'working' class parish but as I reminisce, I can recall meeting only four fathers of my fellow students. Jack Barden's father was a teacher at St. Joe's, where I later attended high school, Jack McNaughton's father was some sort of salesman, who gambled extensively, boozed it up excessively and fancied himself a "ladies man." Pat Lucey and Mike Broderick both had fathers who were frail, ashen, and shy, All other fathers were ethereal creatures, seldom referred to, and almost never seen. It seemed that no father was a 'central figure' in any of my friends or classmates lives. So, while I'm not sure that "working class" neighborhood is the proper description, I do know that no one that I knew had much money, no family was receiving public assistance, and that no one believed that they were poor!

Shortly after the conclusion of World War II, my father terminated his employment with the US Border Patrol and became a salesman for L. Sonnenborn, a paint and building products manufacturer. His territory encompassed a good portion of New York State and Dad spent a considerable amount of time 'on the road', during the next four years.

My personal employment vista improved considerably in August '44 when I became 12 years old and began delivering the morning newspaper seven days a week in my neighborhood for the princely earnings of $4 per week, (if I succeeded in collecting from all of my customers). This job continued throughout my seventh and eighth grade years and once again I was financially self-sufficient. Also, Our Lady of Lourdes school had two bowling alleys located in the basement (cafeteria section) of the building. Through the schoolyard basketball activities during the Summer '45, I became familiar with several of the high school students in the neighborhood, who worked as pinboys at the Lourdes bowling lanes.

During my eighth grade it became customary for these older boys to ask me to substitute for them whenever scholastic or social events made it difficult for them to work their regular shift. Before long I was working one night each week, sticking pins for the men's bowling league, and working Sunday afternoons, between 1PM and 6PM, setting pins for the open bowling sessions. The pay scale was 10 cents per line which meant that I earned three dollars each evening of league bowling and anywhere from two dollars to five dollars on a Sunday afternoon.

Entertainment opportunities were plentiful. There were three neighborhood movie houses in close proximity, and even the eleven or so downtown movie theaters were within walking distance of my home. Dating began in 7th grade and I recall several occasions walking to downtown shows with either Margie Stolz or Mary Pratt.

Buffalo's outdoor sporting arena was located only a few blocks from where I lived. Civic Stadium was the site of college football games, professional boxing, and was the home of the All American Conference Buffalo Bills. Even midget car races and rodeos were held in the stadium. Surrounding Civic Stadium was a large playground and swimming pool complex. All of this had been constructed by the federal government during the Great Depression on the site of an abandoned quarry. We used the city owned playgrounds for softball games and we occasionally used the single wall handball courts. Even though the complex housed an excellent diving pool, large swimming pool and wading area, I never knew anyone who went swimming there. It wasn't that the complex wasn't used,—my friends were simply not swimmers. Of course, when athletic or sporting events were held in the stadium, it was relatively easy for a young lad to sneak in or simply outrun an usher or gatekeeper. We attended events at Civic Stadium regularly, yet we seldom purchased an admission ticket. As a matter of fact, I saw much of the cast of the movie "On the Waterfront" box at Civic Stadium. In the 1940's, Buffalo was a good boxing town and a great Mecca for college basketball.

Our Lady of Lourdes had an outdoor (asphalt) basketball court adjacent to the school building and the second floor of the school contained a stage and very small auditorium/basketball court. Basketball was the passion of neighborhood boys. During the Spring/Summer/Autumn months, Lourdes Schoolyard was the site of choose-up basketball games (full court or one or two half court games). I began playing basketball in seventh grade and my first memories are of me sitting on the sidelines waiting for one of the older boys to get injured, to tire, or to have to go home. The schoolyard athletes were composed of mostly high school students, with several varsity basketball players among them, a few college students, and as many as six World War II Veterans. I was a tall kid and therefore I was sometimes "chosen" as a member of a team, but it was a harsh classroom in which to learn a craft. The hierarchy rules were: "<u>Never</u> allow the man you are guarding to score" and "If you don't know what to do with the basketball, give it to someone who knows what to do!"

Class sizes at Lourdes parochial school were extremely small and in most cases the nuns taught two grades (i.e.) fifth and sixth, each year. However, we seemed to learn. I remember several of my classmates as being quite bright and intelligent. As a matter of fact, each year the two premier boys' Catholic High Schools, Canisius High and St. Joseph's Collegiate Institute held entrance examinations for eighth grade boys and each school awarded scholarships to the four students with the highest test scores. In 1946, although Our Lady of Lourdes graduated only nine boys, four of us were ranked in the top 25 test scores at each school. (I was 8th at Canisius and 14th at St. Joe's).

With plenty of pocket money from my odd jobs, my burgeoning basketball talents, an awakening to the attractiveness of the opposite sex, and effortless progress in the classroom, I really didn't know how my life could be improved, and I certainly wasn't looking for any 'change of scene'.. So, I was greatly surprised and a little puzzled when my father announced that our family would be spending the Easter holidays, visiting his family in Sault Ste Marie, Michigan. My surprise was due to the fact that my father seldom talked about, or to his 'Soo" relatives and I supposed that family relationships would always remain 'frosty' and distant. I also wondered what had caused this sudden change of heart, since my Dad hadn't even attended his father's funeral the prior year.

But in early 1946, my father had obtained a salesman's job and had purchased a new automobile, a Studebaker. To this day I'm not sure whether Dad was homesick, was celebrating his new occupation, or simply wanted to test, or show off his new automobile. I was mildly curious about my Dad's family, and I was anxious to see what the 'Soo' was like, (the only place that I had visited, outside of Buffalo, was West Palm Beach, Florida, which had been a very pleasant experience). Since I hadn't been given the option of remaining at home alone, I looked forward to a few days of 'living on a farm'.

My memories of this trek are quite hazy, but we must have left Buffalo on Wednesday evening to drive across the Province of Ontario in order to reach the ferry crossing the Mackinaw Strait early on Holy Thursday morning. Once the Straits of Mackinaw were navigated it was only a fifty-six mile trip, up a two-lane road, to my father's birth place. I remember clearly that my first, and lasting impression of Sault Ste Marie, Michigan was one of horror! As we approached the town, modest farm houses and single family homes began to appear. There was a schoolhouse, and a church and then we were in downtown. It looked like something out of a Johnny Mack Brown western movie. Downtown was less than two blocks long, with a hardware store, a dry goods store, a five and dime, a Ford dealer and gas station, a diner, a saloon, and a movie theater. I asked that the car be stopped so that I could check the movie schedule and found that the theater was only open on weekends! The rest of the territory seemed to contain only windswept open fields and a few, scattered and desolate, farmhouses.

When we got to Grandma Murphy's house, which was located in the town, I was met by one of the most gracious ladies I've ever known! My grandmother was a large woman, slightly hunched and free of excess fat, with a kind face that contained a perpetual quiet smile, and two bright blue eyes that were magnified by the thick wire framed spectacles that she was never without. As I recall, her first words to me were, "Well Tommy, what do you think of our town? It'll only take you about ten minutes to paint the whole place brown, aye!" With that, she gave me a big welcoming hug and I knew that I had found a lifetime friend. My grandmother also demonstrated a real and very deep affection for my mother. It was apparent in her every word and gesture that Grandma had assigned to my mother a very special place in her heart and in her family.

I was soon introduced to 'Aunt Min', my Grandmother's blind sister, who also seemed to be crippled with arthritis and in need of constant care. My mother later told me that 'Aunt Min' had lived with Grandma for as long as my mother had known my father. I then met another resident of Grandma's home, 'Little Anna'. She was a warm and charming lady, quite petite and much younger than my mother and father, and she had apparently been raised as a 'ward' of my grandmother. Later in the day, 'Annie Brady' stopped in to visit. Well coiffured and attractive, this lady may well have been one of my Dad's older sisters, but she was never referred to as 'my aunt' so I can't be sure of what our relationship was. My mother later told me that Annie Brady's husband was institutionalized, and that the Murphy family never discussed him.

We then got back into our car and went out to meet some of the others in the Murphy family. We first stopped at the farm of 'Aunt Mary', another of my father's older sisters.'Aunt Mary' was another large, sturdy farm woman, who looked to me like she had been birthing calves, milking cows, and steering a team of mules all of her life. I don't remember meeting her husband or her children, but everything was beginning to blur on me by this time. Our next stop was at 'Aunt' Kate's farm. It was deja vu! 'Aunt Kate' looked and sounded just like 'Aunt Mary'. The farmhouse and the barnyard looked and smelled just like Aunt Mary's place. I don't remember any husband or kids!

I only know that I was told that I was going to spend the night at Aunt Kate's. I have no idea where my mother, my father, or my sister Patricia, spent that evening! I only know that I spent one of the worst nights of my life at Aunt Kate's farm. I hated the muddy yard, the animals, the odors, the food and the cot that I slept on. Any illusions that I might have harbored about life on a farm disappeared in one night's stay. I fully understood, and sympathized with my Dad's decision to run away from home as soon as he could. When I was picked up the following morning, I announced that I wasn't staying on a farm ever again! My father laughed and said that he understood my feelings.

On Good Friday we visited my 'Uncle Jack' and his family. Jack Murphy was the oldest Murphy boy and the family favorite. He was of average height, with dark, wavy hair, a bright smile and a constant gleam in his eye. Jack was a policeman, but always seemed in good humor. His wife, Alma, was a beautiful and charming woman, who seemed to be liked by all of the family. I stayed with this family on Friday and Saturday nights, and got to know and like my three cousins, Don, Mike, and Owen Dennis (aka Tuffy), all of whom were younger than I. In fact, I remember that Don and Mike Murphy accompanied me to the Saturday matinee at the local movie house, where we saw Cornell Wilde starring in "The Bandit of Sherwood Forest".

By noon on Easter Sunday I was anxious to begin the arduous motor trek home. I had my fill of 'life in the country' and wanted to resume my days of labor, basketball, movies, and occasional scholastic studies that had become my daily, and enjoyable routine. Graduation from Our Lady of Lourdes School was less than two months away.

My choice of high schools was St. Joe's. It was located only two blocks from my home and all of my basketball playing friends were either students or graduates of SJCI. However, the annual tuition at St. Joe's was $125 and my father had informed me that if I wasn't able to earn the money for tuition, I'd have to attend

Fosdick Masten, the neighborhood public high school. Nevertheless, I submitted an application to St. Joe's and was accepted for Sept. '46 enrollment as a freshman. In June '46, I graduated first in my class at Lourdes and I began work as a soda jerk at Ryan's Drug Store, the first week after graduation. Forty hours per week at 40 cents per hour was enough to allow me to pay my year's tuition and still maintain my "bon vivant" life style in the evenings.

In September '46, I had to resign from the soda jerk position in order to attend school. In a stroke of good fortune, the first week of school, I was contacted by a friend of mine (a senior at St. Joe's) who told me that the owner of the boarding house next to SJCI needed someone to stoke the furnace twice a day and take ashes out twice a week, during the winter months. I faithfully performed these tasks for my four years at SJCI. Here I was, still a coal stoker (remember Mr. Salmon?) but at least my wages had increased 50 times from what I had earned six years before. I was now earning $5 per week. Plus, I was occasionally still getting pin setting duties. More importantly, I was never again without employment until my retirement at age 60.

My father relished telling the story of how he, and his two brothers, ran away from home and came to Buffalo to find work, when they were only teenagers, Only now can I now acknowledge, if only to myself, that in June 1946, I also 'left home'. Although I continued to sleep at 35 Coe Place, I assumed my independence from parental influence, and even from parental custody, as soon as I obtained full time employment. From then on, I went where I pleased and did what I wanted. There was no contentiousness between me and my parents, both of whom I held in my highest esteem. I simply didn't really know them well, and I knew that they didn't know anything at all about me! While I always tried to be careful not to disgrace the family name in any way, I was also constantly and consistently aware that only I would suffer the consequences of any misalliance or of any of my illegal, immoral, or rash misadventures.

It would make for much more interesting reading from here on, if I were to report scandalous adventures, or secret vices, for which I am now either proud or contrite. But by almost anyone's standards I've lived a relatively sin-free existence and even if my life has not been sin—free, I remain unrepentant.

2

MY TEENS

"My imagination, my love and reverence and admiration, my sense of the miraculous, is not so excited by any event as by the remembrance of my youth."

—Henry David Thoreau

What is most startling about the next few years is that they are so memorable,—so much seems to have happened,—lifetime unions were made and habits and attitudes formed which distinguished me for the balance of my life.

My life really began on the day that I walked up the driveway to take my first classes at St Joseph's Collegiate Institute. From then on I relished every day spent at school,—it became my home, my athletic club, my social center. Here I met a group of boys who in four short years would be molded into engaging, respected, and respectable young men. I would affectionately remember hundreds of them for the rest of my life. A few,—Dick Hehir, Bill Poorten, Don Spring, Bucky Illig—became my mentors, role models and close personal friends.

And then, there was my "band of brothers"—Dan Jachimiak, Pete Irwin, Eddie Killeen—who along with Pete's sister—Carol Irwin—became my family and my lifeline. This cadre was my <u>only</u> confidantes, my constant companions and teammates, my muses, comforters and protectors, for my full four years of high school. They, along with my wife, Barbara, continued to counsel and inspire me to goodness, right up until my senility.

In 1946, St Joseph's Collegiate Institute was a small, college preparatory high school, with a history of academic and athletic achievements. Enrollment was between 400–450 students, with class sizes of slightly less than 50 students per class. The faculty was comprised principally of Christian Brothers, with a few lay teachers filling the personnel gaps. The school's motto was "Builders of boys, makers of men." The principal method of discipline was corporal punishment.

The teaching methods which were employed seemed to be standard each year and in each course. The initial few weeks of class was spent learning formula, maxims and vocabulary with elements of parsing and declension. Then, the balance of the school term was spent practicing taking (New York State Regents) tests. So, that while I took four years of Latin, I never read any of the writings of Caesar, Cato, or Cicero. While I took three years of French, my conversational abilities were limited to a few words or phrases at a time.

The majority of the Christian Brother teachers were young (not much older than the students) and from the New York City area. It was quite obvious that many of these young men had chosen the religious life (with its vows of poverty and obedience renewable every four years) to a hitch in the Army during WWII. Some of the younger Brothers demonstrated strong sadist tendencies, but in four years time, I only recall three instances where students were 'beaten up'. I think that most of us accepted a slap or a punch as a suitable punishment, and preferable to several hours of punishment duty—translating Latin, or writing on a blackboard, or sitting in silence.

At the present time we are deluged with news of abuse by pedophiles and sexual indiscretions of religious, political and business leaders. I was an altar boy at Our Lady of Lourdes and served into my mid-teens. I was a practicing, if not a devout, Catholic for my first forty-five years. I was aware that the religious orders harbored some pedophiles, sadists, homosexuals, alcoholics, and adulterers, just as I presumed existed in the military, police and prison populations. But, I never suffered physical or sexual abuse and I never knew anyone who did. I never had any conception that abusive, or lustful behavior was pervasive in our society. And, I thought that I was one of the very few who was aware of the occasional and infrequent moral lapses by some of our most respected personages.

A few of the (older) Christian Brothers had homosexual leanings. But, while these men obviously delighted in the social presence and in physical contact with young men, I never experienced, nor did I ever hear of any sexual transgressions at, near, or associated with St Joe's.

Superior athletic performance was the hallmark of St. Joe's. Outstanding sport teams and individual athletes were produced year after year, despite the complete absence of training (practice) facilities and a coaching staff that bordered on comical. In my first weeks at the school, I was standing in the first floor corridor, when I was startled to see boys in shorts and tee shirts running across the hall at the end of the corridor. Someone said, "oh, there goes the track team practicing." Sure enough, when I went outside, I saw a string of boys running around the small brick building. At the rear end of the structure, runners would enter the side door, climb three or four steps, sprint along the 30' hallway, descend three or four steps, depart the building by using the opposite side door and continue running their laps.

One half of the third floor of the school building was St. Joe's gymnasium. The basketball court was so small that the 'top of the key' circles at each end nearly abutted. Steel girders supported the roof and was so low that any basketball shot from beyond the keyhole area would strike the overhead beams. Of course, all of us developed shots that arched over and between the support beams to the basket rim, but such shots had minimal value in competitive contests. All SJCI home basketball games were played in Canisius College's Villa (field house), not in the SJCI Gym that we knew so well.

After a 'flashy' freshman start, I settled into a 'blue collar worker role' in St. Joe's basketball. I played two years of varsity basketball, following the dictums, "Never allow the man you're guarding to score" and "Give the basketball to someone who knows what to do with it" and I was privileged to play with men who knew what to do when they got the ball. The SJCI teams that I played on produced a total of seven "All Catholic" players and six men who went on to play NCAA Division I basketball. I loved every minute of practice, each and every game,—regardless of how many minutes I played, and the comradery that existed on and off the court.

Social life during the high school years centered around sports events and movies. High school football games were played on Friday evenings, while college games were held on Saturday afternoons. We, of course, attended the St. Joe football games and occasionally watched Canisius College or St. Bonaventure University play at Civic Stadium. On one occasion, I remember visiting the Niagara University Campus to watch the 'Purple Eagles' play football. Basketball season extended from shortly before Thanksgiving to the first weeks in March. The Catholic league played games on Wednesday evenings and Sunday afternoons. College basketball doubleheaders were played each Saturday evening in Memorial Auditorium. We seldom missed attending doubleheaders at the Aud.

Occasionally, after home basketball games, we would take dates to dinner, dancing and a little romantic cuddling. (Yes, even then there were groupies, albeit non-sexual). On Friday evenings, all over the city, various Catholic parishes held CYO dances,—really social mixers. None of my crowd were avid dancers, so our normal routine was to attend a movie, then go to a dance, dance the last dance or two before offering to escort some lass home, (usually followed by a drink or two, and more romantic cuddling).

All through high school, we had "girl friends" whom we asked to proms, or a summer concert, or to a movie, usually on a double or triple date. Here I should state that "sex" played no role in our social life in high school. I was unaware of any boy, or any girl, going beyond the "petting" stage of physical or emotional involvement. During four years of high school, Pete Irwin regularly dated Carol Sequin or Sue Deckop (both beauties), Danny usually escorted Gerry Sherman, and I was quite enamored by Jane Frank. One difficulty that I experienced was that while Jane was attractive, wealthy, and intelligent, she could barely abide my presence,—and I did little to assuage her viewpoint. However crippling this was to my romantic inclinations, Jane remained a good and close friend, and even became "Godmother" to my daughter Maureen.

I began having an occasional "beer or two" during eighth grade and my social drinking habit became more frequent and regular during my high school years. Almost any social occasion was marked by the consumption of alcoholic beverages., It seemed at the time to be almost a social requirement. I never developed any 'need' or alcoholic dependence, nor did I ever feel that I needed an emotional 'boost' or the need to drink in order to relax me or to soothe my nerves. I didn't need a drink to be comical, romantic, or brave. In other words, I was only conforming to my image of a 'hip' young man and I liked the way beer, scotch, and a large variety of mixed drinks tasted. However, whenever I overindulged, I became nauseous. During my teen years, dozens of social occasions were marred by my upset stomach. Vomiting invariably dampens entertainment values, romantic inclinations, and civil discourse, and my companions, friends and loved ones were embarrassed and repulsed countless times by my brutish behavior. My egotistical response to the problem was to switch my preferred drink to 'scotch on the rocks', which didn't make me nauseous. The truth is that I wish that I had never taken a drink of alcohol. It now seems to have been a waste of time and money and only diminished hundreds of occasions and events that would have been more joyful, or pleasantly memorable, without the intrusion of 'booze'.

I have never tasted, tested, tried, or ingested an 'illegal' drug or narcotic. I did poison my body with cigarettes for more than thirty years, but I never wanted to take anything into my body that would cause me to lose control over my emotions, or my senses. Despite the common knowledge of how easy it is for one to obtain illegal 'dope', the only occasion where a narcotic was offered to me was in Yankee Stadium, during a game, when a young bearded man in the seat next to mine, asked me for a cigarette and when I gave him a Marlboro, and lit it for him, offered me a 'free joint' of marijuana in gratitude. I declined his kind offer. Other than that one time, I didn't know where to buy 'stuff', nor did I ever attend social gatherings where recreational drugs were openly enjoyed.

Throughout this narrative, time and again, I've referred to my attendance at the movies. It's fair to say that during the 1940's and 1950's, the Hollywood studios and dramatists were my major source of entertainment, provided me with historical perspectives, and instructed me in the social graces, as well as morals and ethics. Instruction on how to be a loving and responsible husband and fathers were everywhere: (Walter Pigeon—"Mrs. Miniver"; Donald Crisp—"How Green was my Valley"; Frederick March—"Best Years of our Lives" and "Desperate Hours"; Spencer Tracy—"Father of the Bride";) to name but a few. And, of course despicable behavior received its just deserts: (Spencer Tracy—"Edward my son"; Louis Calhern—"Asphalt Jungle"; Montgomery Clift—"A Place in the Sun and The Heiress"). Business ethics were promoted in "Executive Suite"; "All My Sons"; "The Setup"; and "It's a Wonderful Life." Clark Gable, Cary Grant, Gregory Peck and William Holden, in their movie roles, taught me how to dress appropriately, the social graces, and the proper techniques of lovemaking and romance. I learned more about 'command decision' and 'executive leadership' from the movie "Twelve O' Clock High" than from any other source and I emulated the attitudes of General Frank Savage (played by Gregory Peck) throughout my various careers and employments. During my teens, my favorite actors were Cary Grant, William Holden, Marlon Brando and Montgomery Clift. I think that Ingrid Bergman had the most beautiful screen presence of any actress—ever. Other favorites of mine were Ava Gardner and Rhonda Fleming. My list of underappreciated actors would include Frederick March, Eleanor Parker and Arthur Kennedy. I believe that the best movie I've seen was "On the Waterfront."

Each summer, while school was not in session, I obtained full time employment. One year I worked as a landscaper, installing and maintaining lawns and gardens. Another summer I was a stock boy at a large grocery store. Finally, between junior and senior years, and sometimes during my senior term, I worked as an applicator of concrete floor hardeners and sealants. During my senior year my father became the vice-president of a large painting contracting firm and I was able to get weekend work cleaning brushes and drop cloths and doing odd jobs around the shop. In this manner, I was able to accumulate sufficient funds with which to pay my school tuition, my incidental expenses and to finance my penchant for the cinema and an occasional date.

No recount of my high school years could be complete or accurate without acknowledgment of my debt to Buz and Kay Irwin, Pete and Carol's parents, for the kindnesses and generosities extended to me throughout my teens, and indeed for as long as they lived. The Irwins possibly modeled their lives on Nick (Thin Man) and Nora Charles. Both couples were handsome, wealthy, urbane, and perpetually in a party mood, with a cocktail always in hand. The gracious Irwin home was a perennial 'open house' and at all hours of the day and night one could find the Irwin's friends, relatives, and plain hanger-ons partaking of the Irwin's food and drinks and hospitality, sometimes when the Irwin's weren't even at home. I was as big a parasite as anyone! At the Irwin residence, I sought and found food, drink, often shelter, and whenever I needed a woman's friendship or a gracious presence, Carol Irwin's comforting shoulder. For the most part, both Buz and Kay seemed to genuinely like me, often finding my antics to be amusing and being unfailingly tolerant of my sometimes boorish behavior or intrusive actions. Neither counseled nor criticized me, yet I came to believe that they would support me in any endeavor or under any circumstances. I did not consider Mr. and Mrs. Irwin to be my surrogate parents but rather my closest adult friends. The following story perfectly expresses our relationship.

One evening, after a basketball game, Pete Irwin, Dan Jachimiak, and I, took three girls out for "a late night drive". Pete's date was Patty Brinkworth, a 1940's version of "Madonna". Danny was with a 'Suzanne Pleschette' look-alike, Patricia Maurin. I was accompanied by a tall, willowy, 'Lauren Bacall' clone, named Betty Allard. We were in Pete's mother's car, Pete and Patty in the front, and Dan and I, with our dates in the rear seat, when we decided to go out to the "Hacienda" for food and some dancing. "Hacienda" was a 'roadhouse' type bar located on Sheridan Drive, near Millersport Highway, and was about three miles past the city-line and public transportation.

I immediately lip-synched to Danny, "Do you have any money?"

He whispered, "A buck-thirty five!"

I motioned that I was 'broke'.

Dan leaned over to whisper in my ear, "Don't worry, Pete always has money!"

"Hacienda", dark and romantic, had a series of large booths, situated around a very small dance floor. This night, music was provided by a 'jukebox', for there was no 'combo' or other live musicians on the scene. When we arrived, there were three or four other couples, or groups occupying booths.

Once we were nestled into our booth, I immediately ordered a 'draft beer' for me and Betty asked for a soft drink. I then heard Danny say, "I'll have a steak sandwich, with french fries, and a bottle of 'Bud'". His date then piped up, "I'll just have a hamburger with fries, but I'd also like a '7&7' (Seagrams Seven Crown mixed with Seven-Up)". Not one to be outdone, I said to the waiter, "Forget my beer! Bring me whatever he's having!" The tension was broken, Betty gave a sigh of relief and stated that she too wanted a hamburger and a 7&7, but with no french fries.

Pete and his date ordered some food, (Pete never drank alcoholic beverages), and the party was on.

At around 1AM, after several more rounds of drinks, and a little dancing, I mentioned to Pete, while he was dancing, that neither Dan nor I had any money. Pete stopped short and with a tremor in his voice, said to me, "I've only got a couple of dollars! I was expecting that you guys would cover for me!"

I began calming the poor wretch. I said "Don't worry! You and Patty get out of here. Go home and get some money! I don't care if you have to sell your mother's jewelry! But get back here before these guys start breaking our thumbs!" I then returned to the booth and ordered another round of drinks, while assuring Danny that everything was under control. By this time, our two damsels were snoozing in each others arms.

About an hour later, a burly figure hovered over our booth. "Either of you guys Murphy?" the bartender grunted. "I am", I gulped. He smiled and said "Phone-call!". Of course it was Pete. "My dad won't let me come back!" he said tiredly. "Put your father on the phone" I said.

"Well, it looks like I really got you this time, Murphy" was his greeting. I could picture the mischievous grin on Buz face as he spoke.

"You certainly do! What does it take to get us out of this?" I replied.

"Put up and take down the storm windows each season, and shovel our walk for the entire winter" he bargained.

"We'll take down the storm windows in the Spring, and I'll see that the snow gets shoveled when it needs it, but I can't guarantee anything for next Autumn" I countered.

He laughed and said, "It's a deal. I'll send Pete right out to get you".

"A friend in need, is a friend indeed!" and Buz Irwin was my friend every time I was in need!

I gave only the slightest consideration to a selection of college, or to a future career choice. I felt inclined toward a career in law and had thought that I probably would attend Niagara University. However, early in my senior year in high school, my father asked, "Have you noticed that your mother is pregnant?" "Yeah, I thought so," I replied warily. "Well, this means that we won't be able to help you with your college expenses, so it's probably better that you don't go away to school,—we'll need your help at home," he offered. "Okay" I said, relieved that I hadn't received any bad news or had my actions restricted in any way.

In June 1950, I graduated from St. Joe's, the Korean War began, I started summer employment as office messenger at General Mills,—and I met Barbara Moore!. Almost immediately, Barb and I began to see each other regularly, and frequently. There were few double dates anymore but we enjoyed many movies, summer concerts, dinner dates, and an occasional walk to the Parkside Candy Company for sundaes together.

On my 18th birthday, when I returned home from work, I found Barb sitting in our living room. My parents had invited her to join in a 'surprise' birthday dinner for me. She had a slight smile on her face, but she was obviously wary that she might be unwelcome since I had stated on several occasions that I didn't celebrate my birthday and that I deeply resented "surprises." But by this time I was completely smitten, for I had long since realized that there would never be anyone in my life more important to me than Barb,—and I was always glad to be with her!.

However, Barb had enrolled at Nazareth College in Rochester, N.Y. Barb's friend, (and my old flame) Jane Frank was scheduled to be Barb's roommate, and the freshman term was scheduled to begin the next week. We promised to write often and Barb said that she would return home as often as she could.

In September 1950, Barb left for Nazareth, Danny and Carol returned to their respective high schools, and I matriculated at Canisius College. I was adrift. On the first day of school, the Canisius College President addressed the freshman class to announce that we "were in the exact same circumstances as the freshmen who entered the school in September of 1941,—none of them finished school,—they were all taken in the US Army". I was miserable, and I don't recall a pleasant day spent at Canisius College.

The singular benefit of my attendance at Canisius was making the acquaintance of Bob Rodgers, who was to become a lifetime confidant, friend, and companion. I had known Bob slightly when he was a student, and basketball star, at Canisius High School, and when we were assigned identical class schedules at Canisius College, we soon cemented our friendship. Bob obtained an after-class job for me, working with him, at his father's welding supply firm. We shared a passion for playing pinochle and gin rummy, we were team mates on a MUNY (post high school) amateur basketball team, and each of us had a strong distaste for college life at Canisius.

True to her word, Barb returned to Buffalo on most weekends, and we often double dated with Bob Rodgers and his fiancee, Dorothy Doyle. However, when Rodgers told me that he intended to enroll at St. Bonaventure University in January 1951, I didn't hesitate to ape his decision. I obtained a seasonal position, sorting mail nights at the US Post Office, and I was able to earn enough extra money during December 1950, that I could pay for the additional room and board fees for the second semester at St. Bonaventure.

The news of the Korean War, and the horrendous experiences of US military forces serving in Korea, permeated the lives and attitudes of young Americans in the early 1950's. I was unaware of any organized antiwar movements, but it was painfully obvious that there was little patriotic fervor for the 'police action' either. The enemy, North Koreans and later Red Chinese Army units, were well trained and equipped, savage, massive in numbers, and in combination with horrific weather conditions, were inflicting heavy casualties of US forces.

World War II veterans (Reservists) were being recalled into (combat) service on a regular basis and the Selective Service seemed to scoop up boys before they could become young men. There were no deferments from the draft for attendance at college, or for married men with less than three children. College students enrolled in ROTC programs were granted deferments from military service until graduation, when the graduates, who were qualified to become commissioned officers, were required to perform two years of active service, followed by some proscribed period of reservist activity. St Bonaventure University offered courses in the US Army ROTC (field artillery) and therefore enrolled Bonaventure students had draft deferments until graduation.

Bob and I drove to Olean to register for classes early in January 1951 and thus began a seventeen-month idyll, marked by a high-spirited capriciousness, and the company of as fine a body of men as I have ever encountered. Rodgers and I roomed together during our first semester at Bonaventure and were joined in "Barracks Four" by John Travers, Joe Graham, Mike Neville, Tom Waters, Bob Delaney and his cousin Willie O'Toole, Joe Fagan, Jack Terhaar, Jerry Desmon, "Rebel" Henderson, and everyone's most unforgettable character—Tom "Red" Hodson.

Our dormitory prefect was Fr. Jerome A. Kelly, master of the English language, and a disciplinarian who was both bemused and tolerant of the innocent hi-jinks of the young men in his charge. Father Jerome was to become my first mentor, as well as a spiritual advisor, and lifelong friend to both Barb and me. Eventually all of our children were to meet and get to know Father Jerome when the family visited him at St. Bonaventure and later in monasteries in the Boston MA area, until his death on my birth date, August 30, 1999.

For most of the students at Bonaventure, it was a first time experience of coupling the sense of personal independence, with a bonding among a group of equally talented, equally exuberant men who shared in the common goal of obtaining a college education and degree. For my part, I mixed a little classroom activity in with a lot of card playing and a considerable amount of athletics, movies, and beer drinking. I returned to Buffalo most weekends to meet and be with Barb and often to work (both in the shop at Empire State Painting and sometimes as an independent contractor, applying concrete floor hardeners and conditioners).

During the Summer of 1951, I worked for six weeks at American Brass, as a laborer, and after a layoff, I began work as a truck driver for Empire State Painting Company, where my father was vice president. It was here that Jules Broderson, President of the firm advised me,—"when you are in the presence of men that you're supervising,—work like hell! And, if you'd like to be rich,—work like hell all of the time!".

During that summer my Grandmother Murphy stayed with my parents for about four months. She wasn't an invalid, nor was she demanding or needing special care, but as a result of an earlier stroke she couldn't prepare her meals or do household chores either. She dearly loved my mother and I never remember any disagreements or disgruntlement between the two ladies. And it was comical and surprising to see how she would scold, correct and chide her son, my fifty-year old father.

Television was her favorite pastime and she particularly liked watching boxing matches. I recall one evening when I sat with her while we watched Kid Gavilan, a Cuban fighter who was the current welterweight champion, throttle "Irish" Billy Collins. Gavilan knocked Collins down ten times before being awarded a TKO. Later Grandma confessed to me, "Tommy, I always cheer for the Irish fellows, but tonight I knew the white boy had no chance!".

And then there was the evening that I overheard my Dad in heated telephone conversation with his sister Margaret, discussing whose responsibility it was to "care for" Grandma next. And I saw that my grandmother had heard the discussion as well. It was a pivotal moment in my life!

Within a few weeks, Grandma Murphy returned to Sault Ste Marie, Michigan, where she died a year or so later. She had lived a full and joyous life. She had given birth to four sons and three daughters, and she had reared at least nine children, including two waifs. She had provided years of strenuous and stressful health care for her invalid and blind sister, and at last, she had lived long enough to find that no one wanted to care for her!

For me, that memory of my grandmother's eyes tearing up, as she heard her children debating who had the greater responsibility for her care, was one that I can never forget. For at that moment I vowed that, "this will never happen to me!". It probably is most revealing that I didn't vow never to let it happen to my parents. It never occurred to me that I had a responsibility to care for my aging mother and father. I didn't blame my father, or his sister, for being callous. I certainly didn't blame my grandmother for being needy. I simply determined that I would never allow myself, nor my wife, to be at the mercy, or good graces of our children, or other relatives. I had always believed that I would be able to support and take care of myself. I had always earned the money for my education and entertainment. Now I was determined that when I married, my first priority would be the long term financial security of my wife and myself.

On my 19th birthday, (August 30, 1951), I asked Barb to become my wife and we agreed that we would complete one more year of college and would be married late in the Summer of 1952. When I told my parents of my intention to marry Barb, my father said, "Oh, I always thought that you'd marry Carol (Irwin)!". That was the only reaction that I received from my family.

The Moores seemed to accept our decision with gracious equanimity. Yet, as I recall, I let Barb make the announcement to her parents, outside of my presence and without my help.

There was no engagement ring, for Barb and I determined that we needed our money for less frivolous purposes. This was the beginning of our partnership where we saved, shared, discussed, and agreed upon each major issue before any action took place and we shared this confidence for the next 43 years.

In September 1951, my father resigned his position at Empire State Painting Corp. and formed his own firm (sole proprietor) THOMAS J MURPHY & SON. I returned for my sophomore, and final year at St. Bonaventure. This time I roomed with Red Hodson and we cavorted through two full semesters, with little attention paid to decorum, or to academic achievement.

Another aspect of life at Bonaventure that seems strange in today's culture, was the absence of sex, or of sexual activity in anyone's daily life. There was an abundance of drinking and of drunken behavior,—there was scholastic cheating,—there were several incidents of brawling,—but there was little dating or social intercourse with Olean residents at any time. And, if any of my companions, or any student at Bonaventure, ever had carnal knowledge of his girlfriend, his date, or some stray pick-up, I never heard about it, because these things were <u>never</u> discussed, even among the closest friends.

It seems that I have been gainfully employed for my entire life. Starting with the nightly task of putting coal in the Sampson's furnace during the Winter of

1940–41, I had part-time, after-school jobs right up until RCA Service Co hired me as a 'sales coordinator' in 1954, when I then became a 'part-time' student. The money that I earned as a furnace stoker, leaf raker, lawn cutter, snow shoveler, paper boy, store clerk, window blind installer, and finally applier of a concrete hardener, paid my living and entertainment expenses, as well as giving me a 'little walking around money'. For as long as I was a student I used my vacation time to obtain jobs which enabled me to pay my tuition expenses. Usually, I had a job the very next day after school let out for vacations. During the summer vacation months, I was variously employed as a soda jerk, store clerk, construction laborer, office boy and busboy. During holiday vacation periods I tried to cram high paying jobs into the very limited earning period.

I didn't always earn a lot of money. And if the truth were known, while the work was usually hard, I didn't work hard all of the time. I earned the money that I needed. I was never 'fired' or disciplined by any employer. I met some wonderful and interesting people, and I learned a little about 'life'. Here are a few examples—

Landscaping—During the summer of 1947 I was employed as a landscaper by Frank Pike, at the princely wage scale of 75 cents per hour. Frank Pike was a local 'character' with a heart of gold, which he attempted to hide behind a rough and tough exterior, laced with the salty profanities of a longshoreman. He was caretaker of City of Buffalo Park's Department maintenance equipment, and he, and his small family, occupied quarters in City—owned yards on Northampton Street, behind the Post Office building on Main Street.

Pike used his ready access to (unmarked) rakes, shovels, wheelbarrels, brooms, lawn rollers and edgers to garner contracts with homeowners, and small institutions, for lawn maintenance and general yard sprucing. He employed (Our Lady of Lourdes) neighborhood high school boys as his labor force. To describe my employment as a 'landscaper' is a gross exaggeration, for generally I was mowing lawns, raking leaves and picking up dog's 'poop'. Sometimes however, Pike would contract to replace a worn lawn, or to move or replace shrubbery and trees, and on these occasions the work often required long hours, spent in inclement weather, and a lot of lifting, digging, carrying and shoveling heavy materials. I was a particularly prized employee because, though thin as a rail at six foot tall and 160 pounds, Pike thought that I was 'as strong as an ox'. At least that's what he led me to believe! There were some hours where I really earned my 75 cents!

One such occasion was my first visit to the grounds of "The Home of the Good Shepherd". It was a crisp October morning when Pike told Jack Barden and I that he had selected us to work at this "home for bad girls" because he knew that he could trust us to "behave ourselves". In 'salty', but precise terms, Pike defined the type of girls that were confined in this institution, and he told us that the 'nuns' were wary of exposing young Catholic boys to this depraved element. We were cautioned that if we spoke to "anyone" on the grounds of the institution, the three of us would be instantly expelled, and Pike would never again be hired by any 'Catholic' organization.

So it was with considerable trepidation that Barden and I entered the solid metal gates on Best Street, but we were totally unprepared for the sights that greeted us inside the ten foot high yellow brick walls. The interior of these walls was covered by serrated steel wire! Two and three story unadorned brick buildings dotted the extensive grounds. In the center of the property laid a low-slung building that we later learned was a gigantic laundry, employing as many as a hundred girls. Pike later told us that all of the linen, and all of the laundry, for every Catholic institution in the Diocese of Buffalo was processed here. This was an institution identical to the 'home for bad girls' later depicted in the movie *"The Magdalene Sisters"*.

There had been no need to caution us about excessive contact with the girls confined here. Each girl was without makeup, and each was clad in a gray sack-cloth dress and work-shoes, and I don't recall a single instance when I saw anyone smile. I don't think that there was any moment that we were employed there that we weren't under close observation.

Each building had at least one nun peering at us. Some were peeping from behind drapes. Some stood in full view. All made us nervous and wary. At first, a few of the girls would smile shyly, or whisper greetings, as they passed us while doing their chores.(I don't remember seeing any girl resting while I was there!) But gaining no response from their male 'visitors' irritated one or two inmates, and they became surly, uttering obscene invitations and propositions to the pair of dumbstruck teenaged boys

But it quickly became apparent that Frank Pike hadn't selected Barden and I for this assignment because we were trustworthy, but because we were strong, and willing workers. Despite our tension and our obvious 'fear', we worked our butts off. We dug up, fertilized, and reseeded lawns. We cleared brush and trimmed small trees, hauling the limbs and debris across the property to a garbage dump area. At the end of the second day, the air was crisp and the ground hardened by frost, when Pike announced that the only task remaining was to relocate two small trees that were presently situated on the north and south edges of a park, to the east and west edges of the same park. Barden and I threw our shovels to the ground and told Pike, in language which would make the most hardened inmate at the Good Shepherd Home blush, that we had had enough. Pike laughed and said that he thought so too. "Murf,—toss the (200 lb) roller into the truck" he said. When he saw my glare, he gave a raucous laugh and we went home.

On another day earlier that same year, we had finished a particularly harsh day of 'landscaping' at Children's Hospital, located on Delaware Avenue, near Bryant Street. Pike was in the hospital's office attending to some administrative details, when I decided to take his Jeep truck for a short joy ride around the block. Though I was not yet 15 years old, and was not eligible to even apply for a Learner's Driving Permit, I was undauntable. I completed my little trek without incident or discovery, and I drove the vehicle up an inclined driveway and parked it in a visitor's place in the hospital parking lot.

As I was walking to rejoin Pike, I was surprised to see the Jeep slowly back out of the parking slot. I had apparently forgotten to use the emergency brake and then left the gear-shift vehicle in neutral gear. My astonishment continued when I saw the backing Jeep beautifully negotiate a turn and pick up speed as it careened down the driveway into Bryant Street. Fortunately there was no oncoming traffic and the wayward vehicle struck an unmanned parked car before it could do any real damage. It was only then that I observed a pedestrian, his mouth agape at what he had just witnessed, transfixed as he stared at the two vehicles before him. I went up to this stranger and said, "Did you see that? That was unbelievable, wasn't it?" I then suggested that we take down license numbers so that we could report to the police what had happened.

Just then Frank Pike comes running up, all agitated and swearing a blue streak. Before he could do or say something rash, I asked him if he had concluded his business in the hospital. He said that he had and I suggested that we get in the Jeep and leave. Once we got into the truck Pike remained apocalyptic until I told him that I had written down the license plate number of the Jeep that we were riding in and that the pedestrian witness had only written down the license plate number of the car that had been struck "That guy doesn't know who we are! He's staring at the license plate number of the car that was hit!" I said.. As we drove away from the stricken vehicle and the eyewitness, Pike had a broad grin on his face when he said, "Murphy, you really are a smart sonofabitch"

Paint Shop—During the Summer of 1951, I was employed by Empire State Painting Co., a commercial and industrial painting contractor. My father was vice-president of the concern so getting the job was relatively easy for me. But my father never got me an easy job! Here I helped "Louie", a small, wiry German immigrant, who drove the truck and looked after the tools and equipment used by the union painters., Louie and I had to load and unload scaffolding and ladders, clean and fold dropcloths, deliver five-gallon cans of paint to several job sites, and clean (in turpentine) and store dozens of paint brushes each day. Every piece of equipment seemed extraordinarily heavy to me but Louie would hoist barrels of line and scaffolding onto the truck bed as if he was tossing one pound bags of sugar.

Louie had served in the German Army during World War I and had emigrated to the United States after the war. Jules Broderson, president of Empire State Painting, was also born in Germany and he had given Louie a job as soon as Louie had landed on our shores. Louie was extremely grateful to Broderson and demonstrated his devotion and gratitude by working hard every minute of every day, without complaint. Even though Empire State Painting Co was a union shop, Louie had never joined any union, feeling that he had a personal debt and commitment to Mr Broderson.. I worked hard too, for it was a difficult, back-breaking job, but for me it was just a job,—a means of earning my college tuition.

One day the office manager came out to the 'yard' to deliver our paychecks. Louie and I were in the truck, leaving to deliver ladders and scaffolding to a job site. The office manager handed both checks into the truck, and as Louie passed my check to me, he glanced at the dollar amount and his face expressed both shock and dismay!

I was making more money than Louie was! And Louie had put in more than thirty years of faithful service with Broderson! Louie left work immediately that day, crestfallen. He later returned but his enthusiasm, dedication, and energy had evaporated.. I returned to college a few weeks later and I recall hearing that Louie had left Empire State Painting Co shortly thereafter to take a low-paying manual labor job with a construction firm.

From that day forward I never asked anyone how much money they made, and I never shared information about my income with anyone else. All of my life, I presumed that if anyone else could perform my job as well as I, and was willing to perform the job for less money than I was making, that I would be replaced. I never assumed that anyone ever owed me anything!

Postal Worker—Once I received my acceptance to enrol at St Bonaventure I was faced with the need to quickly earn some extra money. The tuition at St Bona was about the same as I was paying at Canisius College but I hadn't anticipated the cost of 'board' when I was accumulating funds for college during the Summer of 1950. Also, with the move to Olean NY, I would have to give up my part-time job at Rodgers Welding, which had been providing me with 'walking around money'.

The US Post Office was the traditional Christmastime employer of vacationing college students.

For two, or three weeks before Christmas, the Post Office hired young men as 'temporary carriers'. The pay was good and the work was relatively easy, if you only had to do it for a couple of weeks. Besides, the regular carriers did most of the card sorting and laid out the delivery routes. But, employment as a carrier for a couple of weeks wasn't going to get me the money that I needed for St Bona. Immediately after Thanksgiving I applied for the job of 'night-time sorter' with the postal service. This position provided eight hours of work, from midnight until 8AM, at good wages, for five days each week, and the prospect of a sixth day of work at overtime, if there was a heavy load of Christmas mail. Besides, I heard that it was possible for an enterprising young man to punch in at the time clock and then find a quiet corner in which to sleep until it was time to punch out and go home. This rumor might have been true, but you couldn't prove it by me. For more than four weeks, I worked eight hours each night until 8AM, then went home to shower, change clothes, have breakfast and report to Canisius for classes and final exams, then spend a few hours at Rodgers Welding, before returning home for a couple of hours sleep before reporting to the main Post Office at midnight. I looked for that 'quiet corner', but I could never find it.

The work itself was monotonous and grueling. Each sorter stood, or hunched, before a giant pigeon-hole cabinet, taking envelopes from a large canvas cart and placing them into individual nooks, which if I recall correctly, were labeled with street names. There was no need to alphabetize, or even to sort by address. Even though there were frequent five or ten minute rest breaks, the repetition made the work exhausting. However, this wasn't penal servitude! We could talk, and smoke as we worked, and there was a lot of 'joking around'. One pleasant memory was the night that I worked next to Phil Muscato, former heavyweight boxer. Muscato, who at one time in the late 1940's had been the 8th ranked heavyweight in the world, wasn't physically imposing, nor was he 'punch drunk', or belligerent. In fact he was a rather pleasant young man! What was most memorable about our meeting was his casual comment that when he was in the ring he "never wanted to hurt his opponent". When I expressed surprise at this remark, he calmly continued sorting envelopes while he muttered, "I wanted to kill all of them'.

In later years, at Christmas time I delivered the mail, and this was a very pleasant way to earn extra holiday cash. In 1951 I delivered mail in the Starin Ave section of Kenmore NY and in 1952 I was assigned routes between Military Road and Elmwood Avenue, south of Sheridan Drive. By Christmastime 1952 I was married and Barb and I were renting an efficiency apartment on Tremont Ave in Kenmore. Barb was working full time at NY Telephone and I was attending UB and working part-time for my father's painting firm. The school was closed for the Christmas Holidays and there wasn't much industrial painting going on at that time of the year, so I signed up for the easy extra money. On the first day on the job, I meet a college student from Vanderbilt University, Joe Perry,—a true kindred spirit. We hit it off, immediately!

The first thing that we did was to combine our two routes into one route. We then divided the route into odd numbered addresses and even addresses. I would take the even numbered homes and Joe would taken the odd numbered homes. We then would drive in Perry's car to the beginning of the route, where he would drop me off with my mail bag. I would then run the entire route, strewing Christmas cards as I went, (we weren't terribly careful about getting the mail to the proper address, we referred to this as 'Meet your neighbor as you exchange greeting cards week'). Joe in the meantime would drive to the end of the route, park his car and begin running in the opposite direction from me, delivering the Christmas mail to the best of his ability. When I finished my half of the route, I would get in Joe's car and drive to where I started, pick up Joe and we would go to breakfast, or go back to my apartment for a nap. It took us less than ½ hour to deliver a route than normally took a man over 2 hours to complete. We performed this routine, three times each day. We delivered an awful lot of mail and still had a lot of time left over for carousing. It was truly a "Merry Christmas" for us!

Independent Contractor—In the Spring'51, while I was home on a weekend break from St Bonaventure, my father announced that he had arranged a 'good paying job' for me. One that I could perform during the upcoming Easter vacation period. He said that Mr Park, a collector of valuable, antique clocks had inquired whether Empire Painting Co would be able to whitewash the basement showroom where the clocks were stored. Dad had replied that Empire didn't work in private residences but that Dad could arrange for an independent, non-union contractor to do the work. That was me! Dad said that I would earn $10 per hour and the job had to be finished before Easter Sunday.

On Holy Thursday morning I showed up at the Park Street residence, located in the heart of Buffalo's 'silk stocking district', Allentown. The 'showroom' turned out to be a large room with mortared hewn stone walls, located in the 'cellar' of an elegant, but very old wood frame residence. There were more than a dozen clocks, ranging in size from 'grandfather' to 'mantel', stored in the dark, dank basement. I began work.

The first task was to move the clocks to one side of the room and set up some lighting to see what I was doing. Then I proceeded to 'whitewash' the walls. It wasn't quite the same as Tom Sawyer whitewashing Aunt Polly's white picket fence! These cellar walls were unfinished and the whitewash poured off the stone, to be absorbed into the mortar without lightening, or coloring the walls to any appreciable extent. I did find that once the first coat of whitewash had dried, it provided somewhat of an undercoating adherent base for future coats. But each successive coat of whitewash only produced a lighter shade of 'gray'. No amount of whitewash was going to produce a 'white wall'.

On Good Friday evening, I had completed work on two walls. I was only half finished and the job had to be completed the next day. I called my cousin, Eddie Ruh, to ask if he would help me. Eddie was a newly wed, who was home for a holiday from medical school, and I knew that he needed some income. Eddie showed up on Saturday morning and with two of us doing the clock moving, and each of us applying as much whitewash as the walls could retain, we finished the job at 9PM on Holy Saturday evening. It really wasn't a job that anyone would be proud of, because "Whitewash' was the wrong covering agent. I'm not sure what would have turned those stone walls white, but I know that no amount of whitewash would do it! Anyway I had completed the contract on time!

I drew up an invoice that showed that I had worked 10 hours on Thursday and on Friday and that Eddie and I had each spent 10 hours working on Saturday. We had actually worked more hours than that, but I was just glad to have seen the last of that cellar and only wanted to be return to the comfort of the Bonaventure dormitory. On Easter Sunday morning I presented my bill for $400 to Mr Park. He looked at it, smiled indulgently and said to me, "Your father said that you would do this job for $100". I reeled, but when I began to protest Mr Park calmly handed me ten $10 bills and said, "You'd better discuss this with your father!".

By the time I returned home I was livid, and determined to take that old scoundrel to court. If he thought that he could bamboozle me because I was 'just a kid', I'd show him what it was like to be in a real fight. When I told my father what had happened, and how I planned to fight this old geezer, he got a quizzical look on his face and said, "I might have quoted him a price of $100". Then he smiled, put his hand on my shoulder, and said, "I thought it would only take you ten hours to finish that job!" I gave the $100 to Eddie Ruh, and vowed that in the future I would do my own 'cost estimating' and that I would never again use my father as my employment agent.

I tried to learn some lesson from each job experience. Overall, I was convinced that I would have to earn any, and all future benefits. Nobody owed me anything, except a fair chance to earn a decent living. I wouldn't be paid more than I was worth, and I would have to demonstrate what I was worth, each and every day. No man, or woman, is indispensable or irreplaceable.

3

MARRIAGE AND EARNING A LIVING

"...for a salesman, there is no rock bottom to the life. He don't put a bolt to a nut, he don't tell you the law, or give you medicine. He's a man way out there in the blue, riding on a smile and a shoeshine. And when they start not smiling back,—that's an earthquake. And then you get yourself a couple of spots on your hat, and you're finished...A salesman's got to dream boy! It comes with the territory."

—**Arthur Miller**
"Death of a Salesman"

Barb and I remained steadfast in our plans to marry, and we conscientiously saved each nickel and dime in order to demonstrate our financial resourcefulness and to achieve our common goal. During the summer of 1952, I worked as a truck driver for my father's firm, while Barb obtained a business representative's position with N.Y. Telephone. We soon settled on the last Saturday of the summer as the most practical wedding day, allowing for a honeymoon extended through a long Labor Day Weekend. Quite by coincidence, the chosen wedding date was my 20th birthday, August 30, 1952.

Even though we were young, our decision to marry in 1952 seems neither rash nor imprudent even as I review it at this later date. Buffalo N.Y. at that time was a bustling blue collar community with a population of more than ½ million people. An industrial mix of steel, auto, and aircraft production, grain milling, railroad and lake shipping, and a thriving construction industry provided a host of well-paying jobs for anyone who was willing to work. At the same time, post WWII prosperity had produced "the man in the grey flannel suit" as new goods were produced and marketed to an eager public, deprived first by the Great

Depression and then by wartime shortages. We had no way of knowing that Buffalo had attained it's economic peak and would be in decline from then on. Had we known this, it wouldn't have made any difference to us! Barb and I had demonstrated over more than a two-year period that our union was eternal, that our combined strengths were much more than twice our individual qualities, and that we were willing to forego current niceties in order to establish a rock solid foundation for future family growth. I was confident that I was strong enough, and smart enough to earn a decent living for our family no matter what the circumstances, and this confidence seemed neither misguided nor foolish.

In the later years of the Great Depression, the US government was still more interested in building cities, rather than destroying lives and property in war. Before the beginning of World War II, the federal government had poured money into the Buffalo area, $4.5 million for public housing, $1.2 million for airport modernization, $2 million for the construction of Memorial Auditorium, $750,000 for Kleinhan's Music Hall, $1 million for modernization of the Buffalo Zoo, $2 million for a new Federal Office Building, $1.3 million for the construction of Civic Stadium, $500,000 to build a new police headquarters, and more than $15 million for the construction of a new sewer system. Not only were Buffalo's cultural and recreational facilities enhanced, but the federally financed construction had provided badly needed jobs for more than 75,000 men and women. During WWII, industrial manufacturing in the area really boomed. Curtis-Wright Corporation employed 43,000, Bell aircraft had 36,000 workers and another 87,000 people worked at three area General Motors plants, producing motors and airplane engines. Bethlehem-Lackawanna Steel became the world's largest steelmaking operation, employing 20,000 workers. Home ownership, or a new car, or a college education, was now viewed as compensation for hard work, not merely the reward for good luck, or fortunate breeding. In 1952, anyone living in Buffalo, who was willing to work hard, could find a good-paying job, and could earn a decent living for himself and his family.

I shared with others who had experienced 'the Great Depression' their fear of poverty and an appreciation for the 'safety net' against personal financial disaster that the US government now afforded all it's citizens. And even though I had been too young to serve in the US Armed Forces during World War II, and couldn't share in the benefits of the 'GI Bill', I shared with the returned veterans the belief that if I was willing to work hard, and obtained a quality education, I would be afforded the opportunity of sharing in the nation's bounty.

There were problems to overcome, of course. By the year 1950, with the return of WW II servicemen, the City of Buffalo housed a population of more than 580,000 in it's compact 42 square miles of land and had become one of the world's most densely populated cities. Barb and I were lucky enough to obtain an efficiency apartment that included a stove, refrigerator, and the use of a washer and dryer, on a nice street (Tremont Avenue) in Kenmore NY, and we were ready for anything!

Initially, we had to deal with the fact that I would be drafted immediately if I didn't continue my schooling. I enrolled at the University of Buffalo for the Fall '52 semester and entered UB's ROTC (Air Force) program at the same time. We decided that Barb would continue working at the phone company and my father agreed that I could continue to work weekday afternoons and Saturdays at the painting concern, while I continued my education at UB. As I recall, Barb and I earned handsome, combined salaries of $74.50 each week and we were sure that we could manage on that amount.

We were married in a beautiful ceremony in Christ the King Church in Snyder N.Y., on August 30, 1952. A few hours later, following a lovely reception at the Sheraton Hotel, we conceived our first child, and we were on our way.

The knowledge that Barb's telephone company employment was to be limited to no more than eight more months and the fact that our apartment, while ideal for a working couple, would be completely unsuitable by the Summer of '53, made it imperative that some adjustments be made in our plans. I obtained a license to sell real estate, but even though I put forth a diligent effort, I was unable to close a single sale in six months. Once again, I signed up for Christmas delivery work at the US Post Office and was able to cache a small reserve of emergency funds. On a couple of occasions, I filled in at Schickluna's Men's Store (Barb's Grandfather) and at a Firestone Rubber Company Warehouse (Barb's cousin-in-law) in order to earn a few extra dollars.

When my father started his own painting contracting firm, he did not go into the enterprise without any sustaining income. He had two or three large industrial plants who employed his (union) painters on an annual contract basis. So Dad had painters working at Dupont and at American Brass every day. But even though large painting jobs came to the firm almost immediately, the income flow was quite irregular and the process of 'meeting the payroll' was a constant concern of both my father and my mother. In all fairness, I was never asked to participate in the business risks, nor to forego compensation in difficult times. Yet my efforts to find alternate sources of employment income were welcomed as contributing to the new firm's well being.

As the weeks progressed, the initial financial instability of the new venture lessened and the coming summer construction season heightened expectations that "Murphy & Son" might grow into a prosperous enterprise. I had expected that during the summer months, as the workload increased, my responsibilities and my compensation would escalate proportionately. Unfortunately, I suspect that my father found these same prospects to be less than exhilarating. Old resentments resurfaced and the prospect of prosperity gave rise to tensions in both of us that neither my father nor I had experienced before.

At all times, Bob and Kay Moore, Barb's parents, were loving and supportive in every way. In the Spring of 1953, the Moores asked if Barb and I would move into a large three bedroom flat, owned and occupied by Tom Moore, Barb's grandfather (age-80+). The reason given us was that "Fod" needed taking care of (cooking, housekeeping, etc.) and wouldn't hear of outsiders giving him help. 'Fod," a seemingly gruff, independent and self reliant old man, dearly loved Barb and I believe thoroughly enjoyed our presence in his home, but the offer from Bob Moore remains one of the most gracious and graceful methods of assistance, and expressions of love, that I've ever experienced. It was exactly the help that Barb and I needed, at exactly the time that we needed it.

Once again, I never expressed my deep gratitude and appreciation to either Bob or Kay Moore, for their generosity, kindness, and love, which was always unsparingly given to each and all of our family members, and in particular, for the unflagging respect that the Moores demonstrated for the love that Barb and I shared.

One evening in May, Barb, now eight months pregnant and no longer working, asked, "How did work go today?". "Great" I replied. "I told my Dad to shove the job and his business up his ass!" "Good!" Barb replied as she took my hand in hers. "You haven't been happy and I know that whatever you do next, we'll be fine!"

I believe that moment was the first that I truly experienced being 'in love' and I have remained 'head over heels' in love and in awe of Barb ever since.

The next day, I went to see a friend, Harry Winters, who owned the local Pepsi Cola Bottling Works, to see if I could obtain employment. I had met Harry in a men's bowling league a few years earlier. He was an affable WWII Vet, who seemed to always like me and seemed to be impressed by me. Harry listened while I described the personal differences I'd had with my father, outlined my educational qualifications and practical experience in business administration, and embellished my experience qualifications in retail and real estate sales. Harry listened with interest and appreciation and then said that since his firm was approaching its busy summer season, they were hiring personnel and could always use someone with my talents. He immediately took me into the plant, introduced me to the foreman, and within one hour's time, I was engaged in taking dirty Pepsi bottles off a conveyor belt and putting them into a mechanical washer. This back-aching work turned out to be one of the best jobs I ever held! The (union) pay was great, my co-workers, all of whom had worked in the plant for several years, and the truck drivers (independent contractors) were hard-working men, yet tolerant of my youth and inexperience. The long, hot summer produced many 12 hour workdays and weekend production, at overtime rates.

On June 4, 1953, Barb gave birth to a 9 ½ pound baby, our lifetime pride and joy,—Thomas Jerome Murphy, and then, roughly three months later, we conceived another infant.

Neither our newborn son, nor Barb's second pregnancy, was sufficient to assure safety from the draft net, so we decided that it was best for me to complete my college education at U.B., get my ROTC commission and spend my wartime duty as a 2nd lieutenant in the US Air Force. I told Mr. Winters of my appreciation for the work, but that I wouldn't be able to continue employment at Pepsi after Labor Day. Harry expressed his regrets that I had to leave, but also seemed a bit relieved, for the Labor Day weekend signaled the end of the soft drink 'busy' season.

It was my first inkling that no matter how hard I worked, or how smart I thought I was, in the commercial world, in the capitalist system, I would sometimes be expendable, and would never be irreplaceable to any employer.

Barb and I were now 21 years old, we had evened out the post-honeymoon rough edges of our relationship, and we were comfortable and happy in our one year marriage and new parental responsibilities. But, more and more each day, I had compartmentalized my life. Student activities were left on the UB campus, neither scholastic problems nor family affairs were to intrude into the workplace, and I tried never to bring work problems or financial concerns into my home. There was also a fourth compartment, my personal, private self. Few people in my life were permitted into more than one compartment and no one was ever allowed into all four compartments.

Late in August, I spotted an ad in the Buffalo Evening News, RCA Service Company wanted to hire a 'Sales Coordinator' to work from 12PM to 9PM, at a location that was exactly one half the distance between the UB campus and our home! Nothing on earth could have prevented me from getting that job! In my sole personal interview I verbally presented my credentials as one who possessed a combination of administrative genius, leadership qualities and 'deal' closing abilities unrivaled in Western New York, and maybe unrivaled even in New York City.

I was hired, and began work on the day after Labor Day 1953. My principal duty was instructing sales techniques to eight full-time television technicians and supervising the sales efforts of two part-time telephone solicitors. The basic product was the service contract which prepaid for labor and parts in the RCA television sets and phonographs. Additionally, I was responsible for answering customer complaints about RCA products and services and gaining customer satisfaction.

RCA had 40 service centers located throughout the continental USA, and when I began my employment, Buffalo ranked 40th in terms of service contract sales and renewals, and 38th in terms of customer satisfaction. After seven months, Buffalo ranked first in the nation in each category. When my school term ended in May '54, I began working a straight daytime shift. I was asked to split my time between Buffalo and Rochester NY, working in the Rochester NY RCA Service Center branch (ranked 34th at that time) two days a week, and I received a raise in pay.

Also, during my final month of the Spring '54 semester at UB, I resigned from the US Air Force Reserves (ROTC), which once again exposed me to the selective service system draft. I had completed all of the academic requirements for qualification for a commission, yet I lacked one full semester of scholastic credits needed for graduation. Also, my new duties at RCA Service Company didn't permit full time college attendance and the pending birth of our second child made my induction into the US Army quite unlikely.

On our second wedding anniversary, (my first year with RCA Service), our prospects were quite promising. Barb and I enjoyed excellent health. We were the happy, proud parents of two lovely children, Tommy and Maureen. At work, the Buffalo RCA branch continued to lead the nation in both sales and in customer satisfaction, and the Rochester branch was now in 5th position nationally. Executives from RCA Service Co. Camden NJ office had come to Buffalo to offer me a District Sales Supervisor position (in Pittsburgh PA) and one of my former supervisors had called to offer a job working for him (selling old movies to television stations throughout Pennsylvania).

I wasn't interested in any of these employment offers since they required our relocation from the Buffalo area. Barbs' family ties were extremely strong and both Barb and I had hosts of friends and warm feelings and memories in the Buffalo area. Besides, my customer relations duties had put me in regular contact with Herm Granite, head of the local RCA Distributor. Mr. Granite had offered me a position selling RCA television and phonographs, Amana freezers, and Whirlpool appliances to retail dealers throughout Western New York. This sales position was more prestigious and more lucrative than any position RCA Service Co. could offer me. However, immediately after Mr. Granite's offer, he became ill and was forced to take medical leave from his position. I don't believe that he ever resumed his management responsibilities at RCA Distributors. About five weeks after our employment conversation, Mr. Granite called me at home to tell me that CBS-Columbia was entering the television set production business, were going to be creating a Western New York distributor, and that a friend of Mr. Granite was going to be named general manager of CBS-Columbia of Western NY. He suggested that I contact Dick Levi and tell Mr. Levi that Mr. Granite recommended me for a position with the new firm.

I met with Dick Levi and was immediately impressed. He was a warm and gracious presence. About 50 years old, Dick was fastidious in dress, soft spoken, cultured, and displayed a personal warmth and quiet sense of humor which never allowed for pretension or condescension. Mr. Levi explained that the CBS distributorship was starting from scratch, with no established retail base or network. Three salesmen had already been hired, V. LaRusso, A. Robinson, and I. Mandel. I was offered the job of District Sales Coordinator (Southern Tier) as much for the ethnic balance I provided as any of my personal traits or qualifications. In fact, while all of the sales personnel had some experience with appliances, only Levi had actually sold television sets. TV was a brand-new industry. There was no color TV, portable TV, or cable TV. In much of the hilly, southern portion of

New York State, where I was to work, TV reception was snowy and erratic, with only one or two channels, NBC and CBS, available to the viewers.

Thus, I became a 'drummer',—a traveling salesman. My new job required that I drive throughout New York's Southern Tier, bounded roughly by Elmira NY and Westfield NY, establishing and servicing retail outlets in furniture and appliance stores, which was the commercial mainstay of every village and small town. It was my practice to stay out overnight no more than twice every three weeks. Even in treacherous, bad weather, I preferred to drive home most nights, even though it was rare for me to arrive in time for dinner.

I never experienced, or viewed any situations as were typically expounded in the 'traveling salesman jokes' that were so popular in those days. Similarly, I wasn't aware of, nor did I partake in any large scale consumption of alcoholic beverages. I don't recall a single instance in which I went out to 'have a drink' with a customer, or alone. Throughout these 'drummer years, I established and maintained close, personal relationships with "other women." My closest friend, outside of Barbara, continued to be Carol Jachimiak (nee Irwin). Over time, I found myself drawn to two others, Evelyn Marinese, who worked at CBS Columbia and Ester Gabel, the beautiful wife of my best customer. Yet while I shared private moments with each of these women, I can state unequivocally that none of our actions were, or could be construed as adulterous, nor scandalous. None of these women had any reason to believe, nor did they pretend to believe, that they were 'my girlfriend', or that we were lovers, or that they posed any threat to my marriage or to my family. I didn't discuss these relationships with Barb, or with my employers or co-workers, nor did my other friends know about these relationships. These were private, as some things before in my life had been, and as many other things in my life would be.

Dick Levi turned out to be a combination boss, instructor and role model. He taught us all how to dress (for success),—yes, salesmen always wore a hat,—winter and summer! Ties (Dick taught us how to tie a half-Windsor knot), suit coats and shined shoes were mandatory. We were instructed where to eat, how to order meals, and proper behavior under all circumstances. However, Mr. Levi gave great latitude and authority to his sales personnel, in order to establish a dealer network. Evelyn Marinese (clerical), Harold Heller (accounting), and Bill O'Donnell (technical), provided excellent support services, to both sales staff and to customers.

Even though the CBS product did not perform in hilly terrain or in outlying areas, I was able to establish strong dealerships in many of the towns in my territory. Some of these dealers, Chuck Mullard in Jamestown, Bob Prentice in East Aurora, and Dick Gabel in Gowanda, became my good friends and staunch supporters for many years to come. As a matter of fact, I now recall that Harvey Schneiderman, owner of Olean Household, and a man that I really didn't know well at all, was extolling my virtues (integrity, industry, etc.) to Joe Crangle, Erie County Democratic Party Chairman, twenty years after I last did business with him.

Shortly after joining CBS-Columbia, I purchased a new Ford station wagon. I recall that in the first 12 months that I owned this vehicle, I put 57,000 miles on it! This epitomized my life while I worked for CBS. Everyone that I knew worked hard. I worked hard and put in long hours. And, hard work didn't leave much time or energy for social or leisure activities. I began playing golf occasionally, but it was almost always business related,—with a customer.

Near Thanksgiving Day 1955, Barb gave birth to our beautiful "Linda," and became pregnant again sometime around Christmas.

Our social life was limited to occasional and infrequent dinner or theater engagements, usually with customers, and once or twice with Dick and Dolly Levi. All of our school time friends were away, performing their military service, and I don't recall that Barb and I socialized with my co-workers at all. I'm embarrassed and saddened to have to admit that I have no recollection of a "family life" at all during my 'traveling salesman' years. I can only imagine the drudgery that Barb endured each day for years on end, as she proceeded, while pregnant, to prepare formula, wash diapers, and clean, feed, and amuse three infants (three years old and younger). I say that I can only imagine how it was for Barb because I know that I was no help to her at all!

For years RCA and CBS had been bitter rivals. RCA, the preeminent manufacturer of television sets, had developed a color producing picture tube and in 1955, had begun televising color broadcasts on its NBC network. CBS, the dominant network, had begun producing TV sets in order to market its completely different method of producing color pictures,—a color wheel independent of the cathode ray tube. Despite the efforts of CBS super salesman Arthur Godfrey, by 1955, it was obvious that the RCA version of color projection was superior and would become the industry wide standard. CBS announced that it would terminate television set production at the end of 1955. We, the staff of CBS Columbia of Western New York, remained and worked hard until the last day of business. Then it was over and we dispersed. What had been a close knit, congenial and dedicated sales organization, simply disappeared.

I had not sought other employment because Dick Levi had been recruited by Hot Point Appliances to join their management staff. Dick had told me that he wanted me to join him at Hot Point and that Hot Point officials had already approved my appointment. When CBS—Columbia closed, Mr. Levi moved to Hot Points' home office in New Jersey. I pretended to join the sales staff at Emerson Television, while I awaited Levi's call to join him. After about six weeks, Dick called me to tearfully say that things hadn't worked out, he was no longer with Hot Point, and there was no position at Hot Point available for me. The next day I went to Cladco Distributors and obtained employment, selling Sylvania television products to my old customers on New York State's Southern Tier.

The transitory nature of the 'drummers' life was now obvious to me, and troubling. I had recently read Arthur Miller's play, "*Death of a Salesman*" and this too had reinforced my conviction that our growing family, and my hardworking wife, needed and deserved both a more stable source of income and my presence at home. When I was working 'in sales', I never gave a customer a commission 'kickback', nor did I ever knowingly engage in 'price gouging' or any fraudulent schemes or practices. I had never suffered the ennui and frustrations of a 'Willy Loman'. Nevertheless, while I had built a cadre of loyal customers, had earned a more than decent living, and still enjoyed selling and the 'travel', I decided that it was time to seek other employment opportunities.

I had only worked Cladco for a few months when I saw an advertisement in the newspaper for a sales representative with New York Mutual Insurance Company. N.Y Mutual was a small casualty insurance company, that specialized in Workman's Compensation coverage. I didn't know anything about the insurance industry, or its product, but the job paid a decent salary and provided a company car, so I submitted an application and was granted an interview in New York City. I was hired and began home office training early in the summer of 1956.

I remember the time of my employment specifically because while I was in training, I confessed to William Dandridge, Vice President of Sales, and the man who had hired me, that I had initially misrepresented my age, and that I was not yet 25 years old. I knew that insurance premiums for youthful drivers (less than 25 years of age) were considerably higher than for the general driving population. I didn't want NY Mutual to unknowingly, or illegally, assume my under-aged risk. Danridge laughed and said that it was all right, I could keep the job, but he did confess that he probably wouldn't have hired me if he had known how young I was at the time of my application interview.

My principal responsibility was to learn the business, under the tutelage of Roy Black, NY Mutual's sole representative in the Buffalo area since the insurance company had been formed. Roy Black was the antithesis of the successful sales-man. An introverted gentleman, of indeterminate years, he was obviously more than 70 years old, but in the eyes of a 24-year old hot shot, he appeared to be closer to 100. Mr. Black never seemed to be interested in training, or in inspiring his eventual replacement (me). On the other hand, he showed absolutely no com-petitive spark, nor signs of resentment, or resistence to my presence. Rather, he appeared at the office each morning, would fiddle with clerical and administrative details and then we would go to lunch together. We seldom discussed insurance specifics, only general principals, but we became friends and companions. We never shared confidences and Mr. Black guarded his province by never introduc-ing me to his clients, or allowing me to accompany him on service calls to long time NY Mutual insureds. I attended Bryant-Stratton evenings, taking casualty and fire insurance courses, and in a few months I passed the State exam and became a licensed Insurance Broker. While I was becoming increasingly cogni-zant of insurance contract provisions and coverages, and was aware of the legal necessity and financial acumen in having adequate coverage, I was never able to discern why being insured by NY Mutual was better than being insured by any other insurance company.

I obtained a NYS license to sell life insurance, and signed a broker's contract with John Hancock Mutual Life, more as a means of filling out my catalog of insur-ance services, than anything else. Almost immediately, I realized an affinity for the intrinsic values of the life insurance contract. Within a few months, selling life insurance only in the evenings and on weekends, my sales commissions were approximating my NY Mutual salary. I was told that Edwin Erickson, general agent for John Hancock, wanted to meet with me. Erickson was an Olympian character, head of the largest John Hancock agency in the world, a millionaire with an impressive urban estate, who often displayed a penchant for pithy pro-nouncements. He told me that he had been following my career and that he had seldom seen such promise of success in a young man. The phrase, "You remind me of myself at your age" sticks in my memory. Mr. Erickson urged me to seriously consider a full time career selling life insurance with his agency, under his auspices.

A few days later, I was offered an employment contract with the Erickson Agency, which guaranteed me a minimum monthly salary which was far more than I was earning at NY Mutual. It also allowed me to retain my Casualty Insurance Brokers License, but stipulated that casualty insurance sales and services must be subordinate to life insurance sales, and limited to part-time. I was told that only once before had Erickson offered as generous a contract to a new agent. That was when Erickson had personally recruited Joe Desmon to become Erickson's protege and eventual successor at John Hancock. Desmon had gone on to achieve monumental success as a nationally renowned life insurance salesman and expert in designing corporate pension plans, but he had broken Erickson's heart by leaving the Erickson Agency to form his own firm. Edwin Erickson had decreed that Joe Desmon's name was never again to be mentioned in his presence, nor at the Erickson Agency. Now I was told, Erickson saw in me what he had once seen in Joe Desmon. I never fulfilled Mr. Erickson's announced expectations for me. I did handily attain all of my life insurance sales targets and quotas and I did become one of the leading sales producers at the Erickson Agency. But, the only way that I imitated Joe Desmon was to leave the Erickson Agency to become Brokerage Manager at the Joseph Desmon Agency, Inc. Edwin Erickson decreed that Tom Murphy's name was never again to be mentioned in his presence, nor at the Erickson Agency.

My years at John Hancock had been productive in many ways. Our family had continued to grow with the birth of our towheaded daughter Kathleen and a robust second son, and fifth child, Michael. And now our growing family required a larger home. We purchased 718 Crescent Avenue and began the lifetime endeavor of restoration and maintenance of a 100 year old, six bedroom, wood frame structure. The purchase of this home was made possible by a gift from Bob and Kay Moore, in the amount of the down payment on the property. Once again, the Moores had provided the Murphy family with the appropriate gift at just the appropriate time in our lives.

718 Crescent Avenue became the Murphy family homestead for the next forty five years. Three children, Robert, John and Meghan were born on this street and this was the only residence that they knew before they established their own family households. When we first moved onto Crescent Ave. the block was distinguished by tall elm trees, which provided a cathedral ceiling over the paved street

and sidewalk, sheltering residents from the summer sun, and all but the heaviest rainfalls. Over the years Dutch Elm disease ravaged the stately elms and the City replaced them with blossoming cherry trees, but the Springtime perfume and beautiful pink flowers were never an adequate replacement for the majesty of the stately elms.

The property also evolved as the needs of the family changed over the years. At first the backyard contained a grassy lawn, with a tire swing hanging from a tall oak tree. Then, one half of the yard was covered with asphalt to provide a basketball court for the Murphy brothers, and their friends. Later, a large above ground, oval swimming pool was installed, which provided many relaxing moments for the entire family. Finally, as the family grew to their teens, a wooden sun deck extended the house's living quarters toward the backyard recreation area, and a flagstone paved patio was added to the shaded area behind the garage. Coincidently, our neighbors on the west, on the south, and on the east, each constructed a 'privacy' fence, in order to partially shield their properties from the constant hubbub in the Murphy recreational area.

Our home was located in St Mark's R.C. parish, and this became the family's foci for social and educational needs. Our neighbors, the Kelseys, the Offermanns, the Lynetts, and the Roberts families became our fast, and lifelong friends. The children soon established friendships that also would sustain them through their school years and beyond. Our oldest, Tommy, met Dan Meegan and they became close as brothers. These two in turn were tutored by the older boys in the neighborhood, Tom Jordan, Billy McMahon, and Billy Ramsey, in the intricacies of athletics and teenage behavior. Our other sons, Mike, Bob, and John, shared the same ages and classrooms with the Werder brothers and eventually a cement-like bond formed between the six boys. Our daughter Linda found a soul mate in Betsy Offermann and it was beautiful to watch these two, shy, brilliant, and gorgeous children relish the other's presence, and quietly share so many precious moments. The Wylagala sisters joined with the Murphy and Offermann girls to form a covey of innocent lovelies on the block.

Our home was located less than two blocks away from Delaware Park and a City recreation program permitted our sons to play golf on this public course during the summer months, without green fees. Barb and I learned to play tennis on the Nichols High School courts, which were only one block from our home and our daughters learned to enjoy swimming at the Shoshone Pool complex that was also nearby.

Barb and I had also formed fast friendships with two of my closest business associates and their wives. We occasionally dined with real estate developer Bob Bradley and his wife Arlene, and we had visited their home in East Aurora NY on several occasions. Phil Schwab was one of the area's most prominent contractors, whose firm specialized in the demolition of large commercial and industrial buildings, site development, and road building. The Murphy, Bradley and Schwab households combined to nourish and sustain a total of thirty children, and our wives thoroughly enjoyed, and deserved, having someone else prepare dinner occasionally.

One of my most interesting, endearing, and rewarding relationships was with the controversial contractor, Philip B Schwab. Phil and I were introduced to each other by our mutual friend, banker Bob Kelsey, and our business dealings quickly transformed into a warm and lasting friendship. I met his charming wife, Marylou and it was engaging to watch the Schwab's marital bliss as a new baby was added to their household each year. There were eventually fourteen little Schwabs running around their huge home at Depew and Starin Avenues. Barb and I would go out to dinner with the Schwabs several times during any given month and eventually I was visiting the Schwab residence on a weekly basis to discuss business matters with Phil.

Phil was short and muscular, giving the appearance of great physical strength. He also had a perpetual impish grin on his face and carefree mannerisms, which masked his street-wise shrewdness and negotiating resolve. He was also a master of diplomacy. I first met Phil shortly after his firm had been awarded the contract to prepare the site for the new Erie County Community College Campus in Williamsville NY. On several occasions I accompanied him to meetings with architects, or engineers, or school administrators, where often the progress of work at the construction site was the principle topic of discussion. Invariably, Schwab was able to cool the hottest of tempers, and satisfy each and every demand and request made of his firm at these meetings. Yet, he never compromised the quality of his firm's work or his personal integrity. And he never surrendered any of the substantial profits or earnings that the contract provisions allowed his firm.

Earlier, Phil had explained to me how he had front-loaded his bid for the rock removal portion of the site preparation work, and how they had discovered hundreds of times the amount of rock that was needed to be removed, above and beyond the original engineering estimate. This estimation error had resulted in massive overruns in the cost of removing rock from the site, the cost of constructing the new campus, and of course, also resulted in enormous windfall profits for Schwab's construction company. The cost overruns also engendered envy from competing contractors, and some anger from some Erie County officials.

After the Community College had been in operation for a few years, the Erie County Attorney charged that the Schwab firm had falsely certified to the amount and nature of the stones used as base material in the construction of the campus roads and parking lots, and persuaded an Erie County Grand Jury to indict Philip B Schwab for fraud. Phil told me that he and his two brothers, young men who had suddenly become very wealthy, seriously considered terminating their construction company activities at this point, but eventually decided that they would continue in business. The County Attorney's charges proved to be groundless, but the adverse publicity of a criminal indictment severely hampered the Schwab firm's ability to raise working capital and the firm was forced to file for bankruptcy a few years later. I had lost a valued client, while Phil Schwab remained my lifelong friend.

It's fair to say that the early 1960's, when I joined Joe Desmon, were good times in America, and good times for the Murphys. John Kennedy had been elected President and suddenly the media was dominated by news of young Irish-Americans, who were bright, honest, and industrious. I found doors open to me that only a few months before would have been slammed in my face. All of our family members enjoyed excellent health, each of our children was beautiful and as a group, they were the best mannered and most fun loving kids that I've ever encountered.

Joe Desmon was an inspirational leader and teacher, as well as one of the most decent man that I've ever met. While I served as Brokerage Manager for Continental Assurance Company, at the Desmon firm, I also studied the nuances of the private pension systems and of estate planning. Desmon was a Chartered Life Underwriter, (CLU is a professional designation which was the insurance equivalent to Accounting's CPA) and he urged me to enroll in the college level courses in preparation for taking CLU examinations. The CLU program consisted of three years of part-time classroom study in the fields of taxation, business insurance, money and banking, estate planning, etc., and successful completion of six examinations before awarding an applicant the CLU designation. I completed the required courses, and passed all exams in eighteen months and became Buffalo's youngest CLU. Later, I also qualified for the Million Dollar Round Table and became the second youngest Buffalonian ever to achieve MDRT status.

Yet, while I achieved some success in insurance sales, and made more than a decent living from sales commissions, I never fulfilled the promise that others had seen for me. I found that I was drawn more toward the management side of the business. Under Desmon's auspices, and with his guidance, I left Continental Assurance to open my own general agency for International Life Insurance Company of Buffalo, a fledgling firm. While I was with the Desmon Agency I had also developed my own clientele, and had become widely known and respected in the Buffalo business and professional community. I also had negotiated a handsome stock purchase arrangement with Harold Farber, principal owner and CEO of International Life, so that it was a financially secure and confident young man who opened the doors of Crimi and Murphy Agency, Inc. in August 1962.

My partner was Cliff Crimi, a longtime employee, and almost a ward of, Harold Farber. Cliff was shy, self-effacing, and as easy to get along with, as any man I ever knew. We worked in harmony and mutual respect for two years, but eventually I tired of representing a 'minor league' insurer. I had lost all respect for Harold Farber's veracity and integrity. Also, I had quickly maximized my profits through a quick and timely sale of my International Life stock. Crimi and Murphy Agency Inc. seemed to be thriving, but I frankly couldn't see any appreciable growth forthcoming, so I offered to sell my interest in the agency to Cliff. After he had consulted with Harold Farber, and Farber had consented, we had an amicable parting. As soon as I terminated my relationship with International Life I was immediately appointed to the position of Director of Estate Planning Services at New England Life Insurance of Buffalo. While this was a high quality life insurance company, and an extremely reputable local organization, ennui with the process of life insurance sales sentenced me to a difficult year in the service of New England Life.

Then, in the Summer 1964, I received notice that I was being called to serve on the Erie County Grand Jury for the month of August. I had never previously served, or even been called for any kind of jury duty, and I was somewhat intrigued by the prospect. My insurance agency was going well, and once I learned that Grand Juries seldom met for more than a few hours each day, I was more than ready to perform this civic responsibility. It would turn out to be one of the most interesting months of my life.

When I reported to the courtroom on the first day of service, the presiding judge explained that 23 citizens had been selected to serve on the August 1964 Grand Jury. He explained that the Erie County District Attorney would present evidence and testimony to the panel of jurors. It was not necessary for all members of the Grand Jury to be present when the DA presented evidence. He also stated that it was assumed that one or more of the Grand Jurors would have prior knowledge, or had even formed an opinion on some the cases that would be presented. Neither juror absence, nor juror prejudice, would 'taint' the Grand Jury action.

The concept was simple: if after hearing the evidence presented, 12 members of the Grand Jury found that 1) a crime had been committed; and 2) that there was sufficient evidence that the accused person had committed the crime; the Grand Jury would return an 'indictment' and the accused would stand trial.

The Grand Jury would hear no 'defense' arguments, nor would any defendant's evidence be presented.. Witnesses to the Grand Jury could be questioned by the panel of jurors and were granted immunity from prosecution for activities which they testified to, although witnesses could be prosecuted for 'perjured' Grand Jury Testimony.

Defendants were not compelled to testify, but if a defendant chose to testify, that testimony was not granted immunity from prosecution. If less than 12 jurors voted 'to indict', the Grand Jury would return a 'no bill' and the defendant would be released.

After issuing his instructions, the judge then said, "I have appointed Thomas J Murphy as foreman of this Grand Jury. Mr Murphy will answer any questions that you may have. Please take Juror's seat #1, Mr Murphy".

I was in shock! Immediately after the other members of the juror's panel were selected, they approached me 'en masse'. There were pleas, "I've got a job, I can't do this for a whole month! Please release me from this duty!" There were threats, "I'm not going to come to these sessions!—and you can't make me come!" And there were a dozen questions that asked, "How do I get out of this?" My answer to all was the same, "If I knew how to get out of this, I'd be the first one out the door! But, I don't know of any escape, so why don't we do the best job we can and get out of here as soon as possible?" Everyone stayed. Everyone took the job extremely seriously. Absences were a rarity. And at the end, almost all reported that it had been a 'wonderful experience'.

At our first full session an assistant DA introduced himself and explained the 'ground rules' of Grand Jury service. He then stated that the August 1964 Grand

Jury was "very important" because the DA's office had been working on a very serious criminal case of "Fraud in the performance of a State contract" for some time, and it would be necessary to present evidence to the August 1964 Grand Jury in order to avoid letting the crime go unpunished, because "the statute of limitations" had nearly lapsed. He explained that if necessary, our Grand Jury would be held over,(past our scheduled termination date) in order that we could hear all of the evidence against the offending 'contractor'.

He then proceeded to present evidence on a series of car thefts, purse snatchings and other relatively minor crimes. We (jurors) dutifully returned indictments and went home for the night. On the following days we were presented with evidence that every crime that I had ever heard of, except prostitution, had been committed in Erie County during the preceding weeks and months. We were presented with evidence of embezzlement, attempted arson, rape (of an admitted prostitute), murder (by four black teens, who returned to the scene to recover some misplaced "shades"), a savage beating of a 'small' man (truckdriver) by two burly white men and two white women after a drinking bout in a waterfront saloon, date rape, assault of policemen by a celebrated running back of the Buffalo Bills (not OJ Simpson), kidnapping and rape (of a teen-age girl attending a 'fireman's picnic' in Ellicott Creek Park), manslaughter, insurance fraud, as well as a couple of bizarre charges of "illegal entry" and "illegal exit".

And every few days, we were reminded that our term would be extended so that the DA could present the 'important' fraud case to us.

Some of the most interesting cases were also the least grisly. For instance, a 'black' teenager testified that on a Friday evening he was walking down a street, when he saw a police squad car approaching. In fear, he threw a switchblade knife that he was carrying, onto a nearby factory roof. When the squad car had passed, the boy climbed onto the roof to retrieve his knife. Once on the roof, the youth saw a 'skylight' and leaned over to see what he could see in the factory below. He fell through the glass skylight, crashing on the concrete floor two stories below, where he laid, with two broken legs, until the plant reopened on Monday morning. The Grand Jury indicted the youth, charging him with "illegal entry". One of the jurors said to me, "I don't care if he's guilty! He was carrying a knife! We've got to get these animals off of our streets!"

The testimony in another case was that a man, on his first time visit to a dentist, entered an apartment which adjoined the dentist's office. The accused stated that the apartment door was wide open and that he thought that he was entering the dentist's office. Once inside the apartment the accused saw a purse on a coffee table. As he picked up the purse, the man heard a woman's scream and he turned to see the apartment dweller in the doorway. He immediately fled the scene, thrusting the unopened purse into the midriff of the stunned woman as he went past her. The Grand Jury indicted the intruder, charging him with "illegal exit". It was my understanding that "illegal entry" couldn't be charged since the apartment door was wide open." Fleeing the scene of a crime" couldn't be charged since no 'crime' had been committed, (or at least instant restitution had taken place). The DA informed us that the man could be charged with "illegal exiting from the premises" After that one we were all anxious to take on the 'serious' contractor fraud case!

Sometimes a case so intrigued me that I followed it through the court system (perhaps to assure myself that 'justice' was served). One such case involved an off-duty policeman walking down a lane in a vacation-cottage community when he heard the sound of glass breaking. His testimony was that as he was looking for vandals he noticed one cottage that had rags, rather than curtains or drapes, hanging in the windows. He looked inside the cottage and saw that the place was ready to be 'torched'. He immediately obtained a search warrant and when he entered the cottage he found that it was empty except for additional rags hanging on hangers in the closets, and plastic gallon bottles of flammable liquid, with fuses inserted, scattered throughout the cottage. The only furnishings in the house was a metal bedstead, with an old, stained mattress, a dilapidated sofa and a plywood dresser stuffed with more rags. Further investigation revealed that the owners of the property had tripled the amount of fire insurance on the property only two months prior to the policeman's discovery. Neighbors testified that the owners had announced that they were leaving on a one week vacation two days before the discovery. The Grand Jury of course indicted the owners for "attempted arson". I kept track of this case through the local newspapers and was shocked to learn that the case was 'thrown out of court' (dismissed) about six months later on the basis that the off-duty policeman did not have 'probable cause'(of a crime) and therefore had conducted an illegal search when he first looked into the cottage window.

The August 1964 Grand Jury had returned 48 indictments during the month. We were still being told that our term was going to be extended in order that we would hear the 'serious contractor fraud' case before the statute of limitations ran out. But first, each Grand Jury is required to inspect County prisons in order to insure that prison officials are conducting themselves properly and that prisoners are not being mistreated or abused.

When we visited Wendy Correctional Facility it was my first look at a prison cell. I couldn't believe my eyes! In the movies, when Humphrey Bogart or Jimmy Cagney were in their cells, usually with other inmates, it seemed as if they were strolling around a living room, or in a small efficiency apartment. A real prison cell is about 8'X10' and contains a washbasin and toilet. There is no privacy and barely room to turn around, much less pace back and forth. And anyone who has heard it, will never forget the sound of a prison cell door being closed! While we were at Wendy, a prisoner asked to speak to the foreman of the Grand Jury. He told me that he had been illegally arrested and was being held without being charged and without trial. When we returned to downtown Buffalo, I went to the Office of the District Attorney to make sure that the complaining prisoner wasn't being illegally restrained. While there I saw a number of friends and acquaintances who were members of the DA staff. They asked what I was doing in the DA's office. I told them of my visit to Wendy and of the prisoner's complaint. Everyone seemed surprised to find that I was serving as foreman of the August 1964 Grand Jury. The next day we were collectively thanked, told that our services would no longer be required, and the August 1964 Grand Jury was dismissed. One month later, I read in the newspapers that the September 1964 Grand Jury indicted my very good friend, my golfing partner and constant companion, and my close business associate, Philip B Schwab, for "fraud in the conduct of a contract with New York State". It certainly is a small world after all!

My Grand Jury service is indelibly etched into my psyche. First, there is no question that the District Attorney is in complete control of the Grand Jury. He decides what evidence is presented, and when it is presented, and how it is presented. He tells the members of a Grand Jury what the rules of the game are and in reality controls Grand Jury actions as if he were a puppeteer. The idea of a "run-away grand jury" conducting it's own investigation, may be legally possible, but is pure fantasy.

Nevertheless, it seems to me that the system not only works well and greatly benefits 'society', but that the grand jury concepts, if applied to criminal trials, would correct many of the flaws which currently hamper the administration of justice. If criminal trial juries consisted of 23 people, randomly selected from a pool, with neither prosecution nor defense counsel given "challenges", the jury selection process would be immeasurably speeded, and all need for 'racial' balance, fear of 'prejudice' or bias, would be eliminated. Only the judge would determine if a juror was unfit or unable to serve on the jury. Jury deliberations would be by secret ballot, each juror allowed to vote "guilty", "not guilty" or "undecided", and a verdict would be reached when twelve votes of "guilty" or twelve votes of "not guilty" was recorded by the jury foreman. This procedure would eliminate 'jury tampering' and would prevent one, or a few, jurors from prolonging or avoiding a verdict. Additionally, this process would free each individual juror from the fear that he, and he alone, could be responsible for a miscarriage of justice.

Secondly, the realization of how terrible incarceration in a prison cell must be, has made me more sensitive to the need to find alternative methods of punishment for minor offenses and certainly less anxious to "get those animals off of our streets'. On a tour of now vacant Alcatraz Prison, the guide stated that in the past, prisoners who had no 'work duties' were confined in their prison cells for 23 hours each and every day. This is 'cruel and inhuman treatment' and I'm convinced that under those conditions, a man would be converted into an 'animal' in a very short period of 'jail time'. I have a few close friends who have been imprisoned, albeit in federal, "country club" like facilities with tennis and 'health club' privileges, so I'm sure that for some the old "chain gang" method of rehabilitation is outmoded. However, when we consider that a very large percentage of today's prison population is serving time for the 'first-time' possession of a 'controlled substance', we might reflect on what kind of future citizens are being created by incarceration.

Finally, all of my senses of personal safety and security have been completely shattered. Before my grand jury service I had complete confidence that I could, and would, survive any criminal encounter. I assumed that if I was robbed, that any robber would be satisfied if he received all of my worldly goods. If I was threatened, it seemed logical that I wouldn't be harmed if I acceded to every demand. I was sure that only resistance would provoke violence! "If rape is inevitable, lay back and enjoy it!" seemed like incredibly good advice. Certainly, no one is so stupid or cruel that they would kill you without reason or provocation. Each of these homilies is wrong! Day after day of grand jury testimony convinced me that there are people out on the street who will maim and harm any living creature, thoughtlessly, without reason, without provocation, or without cause. And because it is thoughtless and unreasoned, incarceration, or other punishments are not deterrents to these crimes of violence.

And by the way, Philip J Schwab was acquitted of all charges of "fraud" and of "perjury".

One other change had occurred in my life at this time. I had a vasectomy operation performed, in order to prevent additional childbirths. By this time, Barb and I had completed the formation of our family. Our sons Robert and John had been born in quick succession and our 'last' baby, Meghan, was born just three days before the assassination of President Kennedy. Barb had performed the remarkable feat of giving birth to, and raising eight infants in the space of less than eleven years!

I really can't recall a single instance when Barb or I resented or despaired over the creation of another fetus, or birth of another child. But when it seems that every sexual intimacy results in pregnancy, the libido of both partners can be severely damaged. The Catholic Church, and our spiritual confessors, were of no help to us, or to our friends. The Church's position on birth control was implacable: No system or device, other than the 'rhythm method' or complete abstinence from sexual activity, could be used to limit the number of children produced in a marriage. I have attempted to relate in these pages how incredibly strong and resourceful young Barbara Murphy needed to be in order to cope with the daily grind of raising a brood of rambunctious infants. Several of our friends visibly cracked under less strain. There is no telling how many marriages, and love affairs, were irreparably damaged by the Vatican's insensibility.

The Vatican's interpretation that any form of birth control was sinful was most despicable in that if one marriage partner determined that mental, physical, or financial health was endangered by additional childbearing, it was necessary that the other marriage partner agree to join in the 'sin' of birth control. One couldn't singularly risk 'eternal damnation' in order to safeguard the well being of a loved one. Rather, one had to ask a loving partner to participate in a 'sinful' activity. This seems absurd today, but that was (and is) the teaching of the Catholic Church. I know some decent people who were literally driven crazy by this Church doctrine. Today, some Catholics say that they can ignore, or are not bothered by this 'teaching' of the Church, but in the 1950's and early 1960's few problems were more troublesome to our circle of friends than the Catholic Church's unbending attitude toward 'birth control'.

During these years of life insurance sales work, times had been surprisingly good. I've often stated that Barb and I, and our family, never experienced a day that was as 'bad' as I had expected our average day would be, when I first proposed to Barbara Moore. Each Murphy child was born robust and healthy and while each had developed their own personality, they had combined to become a harmonious group that looked after themselves and tended each other.

Barb and I had become particularly fast friends of Buz and Irene Roberts. Buz, an attorney, had served as an aide and 'confidant' of former Buffalo Mayor Frank Sedita. In 1964, Sedita had announced that he had obtained the endorsement of Buffalo's Liberal Party, and now was going to challenge the Democratic Party leadership by running in the Democratic Party primary election for Mayor. I told Buz that I would like to help Sedita. Buz replied that a smarter move for me was to work for the election of Tom Ryan as Erie County Sheriff. Ryan was a tremendous underdog, but Roberts reasoned that I could assume a high profile in this campaign for Sheriff and possibly make a substantial contribution toward a Democratic upset.

I then embarked on a three-month adventure that was an exhilarating, entertaining, educational, and uplifting experience, a political campaign. Let me say at the outset that Ryan was running against a popular incumbent, a record vote getter, for a political office (Erie County Sheriff), that was a major source of patronage for Erie County Republicans. All deputies were political appointees (not civil service) and no arrests were ever made! Nobody was mad at the Sheriff! In the November election, we got murdered!

But, every day, I wrote a speech! I designed a questionnaire that polled voters on campaign issues. I recruited, trained and supervised volunteers who made daily telephone inquires. I tabulated poll results. I designed, ordered and supervised the distribution of megaphones (Buffalo Bills games) and Buffalo Sabre hockey schedule cards (which were the first distributed in the Sabre's initial NHL Season). Both products highlighted the virtues of TOM RYAN for Sheriff. I advised Ryan on campaign financing and on all other aspects of this grueling experience. And I made lifelong friends of those others who worked on this campaign: Tom Ryan (later appointed Buffalo City Court Judge and twice elected to the NYS Supreme Court); James Cosgrove, elected three times as Erie County District Attorney and later named by NYS Governor Rockefeller to head the Western New York Waterfront Planning Commission; John Doerr, former NYS Senator, later elected to the NYS Supreme Court, where he served as the Administrative Judge for the Eighth Judicial District.

And of course, I had almost daily contact with Joe Crangle, who was the fledgling Erie County Democratic Chairman. Also, it was during the course of this campaign that I first met Jim Burns and George Wyatt,—both of whom were serving as my counterparts in the successful Frank Sedita campaign. So even though we had lost the election for Erie County Sheriff, I came to the realization that I wanted to do more with my life than sell insurance. The words, ideas, and ideals of John and Robert Kennedy, and of Adlai Stevenson, had imbued me with the sense that "public service" was a 'noble' calling and indeed I believed that the efforts of 'one man' could make a difference.

When Buz called me in the early months of the Sedita Administration, to ask if I would be interested in taking a position in the Mayor's Office, I jumped at the opportunity and immediately gave New England Life thirty days notice of my intention to leave their employment.

However, within a week or ten days after Roberts' call, I received another employment offer. This time it was from Ed Cottrell, USA's largest Ford dealer, a millionaire before he was 30 years old, and a former classmate of mine at St. Bonaventure. Ed called to tell me that he'd heard that I was about to join the Sedita administration and he asked that I first consider another employment option. Cottrell explained that he was expanding his business interests into new areas and he wanted me to join his organization. After some intensive negotiations, I agreed to join Cottrell. I was given a handsome salary, expense account, incentive bonuses, and <u>two</u> company cars (station wagon and Mustang) which dimmed the allure of 'public service'. In return for this largesse, I served as vice president in four separate management firms, where I ran an insurance agency, managed commercial real estate properties, headed a commercial real estate development project, and assisted Cottrell in acting as agent for professional athletes.

When I called Buz Roberts with the news, he was jubilant at my good fortune and our relationship wasn't tarnished at all by my vacillating between "good works" and "great pay."

Thus I plunged into a new work environment, long hours, few holidays, intensive pursuit of the "deal," scratching for each and <u>every</u> dollar, and an insatiable appetite for attaining the 'maximum' profit. I was working for a small town Donald Trump!

In 1952, Ed Cottrell terminated his college studies when his father, a Ford dealer in West Seneca NY, died suddenly. Cottrell returned home to help his mother manage the fledgling family business. Cottrell possessed a natural shrewdness and within a decade he had expanded his family business interests to include a network of corporations that owned four urban Ford dealerships, a bus company that supplied transportation to students attending suburban schools in Western New York, as well as a myriad of real estate holdings.

His lifelong penchant for fastidious accounting, and his learned aversion to investing his own money in any venture, made Cottrell a canny real estate investor. He became a ruthless and relentless negotiator and regardless whether his antagonist was an employee, a customer, supplier, a business partner or associate, or a family member, Cottrell relished the opportunity to advance his arguments into a court of law. He became the type of executive who not only made sure that every T was crossed and that every I was dotted in every contract that he was party to, but one who spent much of his working life finding where a comma could be inserted into a paragraph that changed, or could be interpreted as changing, the intent of the provisions of a document.

In the mid 1960's, Cottrell's burgeoning Ford dealership network had warranted a new and larger showroom in West Seneca to replace the small, rural type building that had served his family's interest since before World War II. Cottrell's initial development gambit was to purchase options for the purchase of a couple of truck farms that were located on Union Road, less than a mile away from Cottrell's existing dealership.. The options, which cost Cottrell only a few dollars, gave Cottrell the right to purchase the truck farms for a predetermined, but very generous price.

The small investment in options reserved the truck farm land for Cottrell's future use and gave him all of the leverage he needed to begin serious negotiations for financing his development dream. Each of Cottrell's four Ford dealerships used M&T Bank as their primary source of automobile financing. This meant that Cottrell was providing M&T with hundreds of extremely profitable, secured loans, and new customers, each month, and made Edward Cottrell one of M&T's most valuable clients. He therefore had considerable negotiating leverage with this financial institution. Once Cottrell outlined how the increased sales generated by a new and larger building would increase the profits of both Cottrell Ford and M&T, the bank readily agreed to finance both the purchase of the optioned land and the construction of the proposed new dealership building.

Then, Cottrell produced aerial photographs of the neighborhoods surrounding the new Ford dealership. The pictures showed earth being overturned all over the area,—evidence of new residential construction! Cottrell contended that, in only a few years, his development site would be Erie County's center of population.. It was an ideal location for the construction of a major retail shopping center! M&T Bank was exuberant over the thought of becoming the financial partner to a young entrepreneur with such vision! Then, Cottrell asked if M&T would agree to construct a branch bank at this location, and in effect become Cottrell's initial tenant. It was Shakespeare who first wrote, "Our doubts are traitors, and make us lose the good we oft might win, by fearing the attempt". M&T agreed to construct a new branch bank building near the Ford dealership, and to pay Cottrell a monthly rental fee for the use of the land. This is when Cottrell hired me!

Cottrell had handled all of the negotiating with M&T, with Ford Motor Company, and with design architects and construction contractors. The concept and design of the project, making the profit projections, and obtaining the development financing had been accomplished before Cottrell had called me. My Union Square tasks were limited to negotiating leases, finding tenants, obtaining options to purchase land, and supervising the architectural and construction activities. Eventually, a large chain supermarket and drugstore were constructed adjacent to the M&T Bank, and a florist, barbershop, liquor store and small restaurant were later added. However, I was unable to persuade either K-Mart or WoolCo (newly founded discount department stores), to build at this site, and major department stores and theater complexes also opted for other locations.

Cottrell's initial real estate development (Union Square) remained a neighborhood strip plaza, but he had established his credentials as a "developer" and he had succeeded in persuading other parties to pay for his new Ford dealership. Furthermore, he had sharpened his negotiating skills and had developed a technique for obtaining development funds for grandiose projects whose chances of success were uncertain at best. It was a procedure and technique that later proved so successful when Cottrell fantasized that he could build a domed football stadium and then sold Erie County on the idea of paying for the construction of the structure, while letting Cottrell manage the facility.

At the end of eighteen months of frenzied activity, and being under constant pressure to succeed with an ever increasing profit margin, I was exhausted,—literally burnt-out.

Barb and I took a respite at the "Inn at the Park" Hotel in Toronto. At dinner, I told Barb that I no longer wanted 'one dollar more' so badly that I would do anything to get it. I described the offer that Buz had made me and I said that since the City Hall position paid considerably less money than I had been making, I wanted to discuss and consider all aspects of our acceptance of the 'less glamorous' civil service status.

There was no hesitation, as Barb replied,

> "Tom, we'll be fine in whatever occupation you accept. Whatever makes you happiest is what 's best for the family. Let's go to City Hall and we'll give them our best shot!"

Once again, without complaint, without any display of self-sacrifice, Barb stepped forward, slipped into harness and demonstrated her total support for my endeavors.

As a result of our failure to obtain a major retailer to anchor the Union Square development, my relationship with Cottrell had chilled, so that when I told him that I was leaving, there was only a perfunctory handshake, a few mumbled best wishes and our relationship had ended as abruptly as it had begun. We never spoke to, or about each other again, except to acknowledge the other's presence at public functions.

Bureaucratic procrastination delayed my City Hall appointment. These ten days of unemployment were the only ones that we experienced in 15 years of marriage. Commission incomes had vacillated wildly during most of the period. At times the family existed on extended credit. During plush times we paid off our debts before making any new purchases. There were times when Barb and I deferred buying anything but daily family necessities, until credit and department store debt was eliminated. Everyone in the family contributed to meeting our daily needs. Each Murphy child was an accomplished snow shoveler and lawn mower. Each Murphy boy obtained a paper route as soon as he was 12 years old. Each Murphy daughter baby-sat the neighbor's children as soon as the girls reached their teens. We had all learned that there were things that we couldn't afford. We also knew that we could get whatever we needed by working for it. There were no complaints, no utterances of dissatisfaction or disappointment. My selling career was over. What lied ahead was a time of intellectual growth, and the opportunity for, and challenge of public service.

4

CITY HALL YEARS

"Let the word go forth from this time and place, to friend and foe alike, that the torch has been passed to a new generation of Americans, born in this century, tempered by war, disciplined by a hard and bitter peace, proud of our ancient heritage and unwilling to witness or permit the slow undoing of those human rights to which this Nation has always been committed, and to which we are committed today at home and around the world."

—John F. Kennedy
Inaugural Address

In the two decades following World War II, Buffalo NY had grown to a population of more than one-half million people. The three principal ethnic groups were Irish, Polish and Italian,—all Roman Catholic. Buffalo was also a 'mob' town and an organized labor bastion, with hourly wage rates the second highest in the nation. Mayor Sedita's first term (1956–60) was marked by published reports of organized crime tie-ins, widespread rumors of the Mayor's romantic dalliances, and a couple of internal theft scandals. In 1960, Buffalo's population had declined by more than 45,000 people from it's 1950 high and several prominent, large employers, including Spencer-Kellogg, DuPont, National Anilene, and Hooker Chemical, had made the decision to relocate manufacturing facilities to other parts of the country. The electorate revolted, and in a political upset, this popular Democratic mayor was turned out of office after four years.

Following four horrendous, scandal ridden years of Republican governance, Frank Sedita was elected to a second term as Buffalo's Mayor in 1966. During the interim term there were some substantial changes made in the way that the City received and disbursed funds. Both New York State and the Federal government were fostering, promoting and financing programs for the development of low and middle income housing, the improvement of neighborhoods (both resi-dential and commercial), community activism in the political and educational processes, and, to a lesser extent, in economic development.

In a radical change from the earlier methods of financing municipal projects, now the Office of the Mayor applied for, and received the State and Federal commu-nity development funds, and the Mayor alone was responsible for the proper administration of the programs and distribution of these funds, albeit within the legal parameter of each program. Neither the City Council, nor the City Comp-troller, had any responsibility for the proper disbursement of these funds. It was a time of awesome responsibility and of tremendous temptation toward licentious-ness. Several of the best loved, most respected, and even hallowed US mayors spent time in prison for the misuse of federal and/or state community develop-ment funds.

By the time Sedita returned to the Mayor's Office, Buffalo's fiscal condition had badly deteriorated.. Under Mayor Kowal, Sedita's predecessor, Buffalo had lost it's federal certification, and funds, because of it's inability to revise and enforce it's multiple dwelling laws and because of the City's sluggishness on urban renewal and anti-blight programs. New York State had decided to construct it's new university (SUNYAB) in Amherst NY, rather than in downtown Buffalo, as originally planned, and there was growing opposition to the long anticipated construction of a new football stadium on Buffalo's waterfront.

Frank Sedita was born to be a mayor. He was cut from the same mold as his con-temporaries, Daly in Chicago; Curley in Boston; and Corning in Albany. Sedita was a natural raconteur, urbane with a twinkle in his eye and a knowing smile on his lips which concealed a Machiavellian mind and unbounded ambition. But he was much more than 'just another local politician'! In his second term in office, Mayor Sedita surrounded himself with a cadre of hard working, loyal, and some-times brilliant, municipal activists. This proud man was determined to restore Buffalo's fiscal integrity and economic well-being, but of equal importance, he wanted to restore and preserve his personal reputation.

Late in August 1967, only a few days short of my 35th birthday, I received my appointment as Project Manager in Buffalo's Department of Community Devel-opment. The City had recently received federal approval of the the Allentown-Lakeview CCE Project. Properties eligible for federal assistance under this new program were evenly divided between Buffalo's West Side (the Italian community,—Sedita's rock solid political base) and the Allentown neighborhood, (silk-stocking Republican) and the Mayor wanted an independent (City Hall outsider) administrator for this high-profile program. This was only the third Concentrated Code Enforcement Project approved in the nation and I was told that Mayor Sedita was anxious that the program be run effectively, efficiently and without the slightest hint of favoritism or corruption.

On my first day in City Hall I stopped in and thanked Buz for recommending me for the Project Manager position. Roberts said, "Thank the Mayor. He's the one who appointed you." I made an appointment and the next day I was ushered into the Mayor's prepotent presence, "Mayor, I'm Tom Murphy and I want to thank you for giving me the opportunity of serving you and the City," I said. The Mayor gaped, and after a moment said—"So that's who you are!" Sedita had obviously received favorable reports on me and he had frequently seen me in the presence of Buz Roberts, but he had never put the reports, and the name, and the face together.

On that day Mayor Sedita and I initiated a close relationship that spanned more than a decade. We were never close friends, but we shared a mutual respect for the integrity and competence of the other. We shared more private moments than public spotlights. I can state categorically that Mayor Sedita never ordered, requested, or suggested that I do anything against my conscience, and I never knew Mayor Sedita to perform an illegal, criminal, or immoral act or action.

My years of government service were to become a delight. At City Hall I met and enjoyed the friendship of an outstanding group of bright, hard working, and dedicated young men. Certainly, my 'last' mentor, Judge H. Buswell Roberts, was also my best friend. Of all of the people I've known, Buz was the only one that I found to be faultless. I was often dissuaded from reckless actions and activities by the specter of tarnishing my image in Judge Roberts' eyes. Buz had a mastery of language and of logic. He was compassionate, he could be critical, but I never knew him to be condescending.

Jim Burns, Commissioner of Administration and Finance, was an acerbic student of governance and a brilliant tactician in the art of municipal fiscal practices. He was unfailingly loyal to his mayor, the Democratic party and to his administrative responsibilities. Above all, Jim was a steadfast friend.

Dick Miller, Commissioner of Community Development, was an affable presence, meticulous in administrative duties, but impervious to structured schedules, appointments, or time constraints. Dick was literate, scholarly, unrestricted by political motivations or financial need, scrupulously honest, and compellingly dedicated to the improvement of urban conditions.

George Wyatt, Municipal Housing Director, was warm, generous and passionate in all that he did. He couched each problem, each opportunity, and each question in socio-political terms and prospective. And nothing would dissuade George from speaking and acting in behalf of the 'Black' community, the poor and oppressed people living in Buffalo, and all underprivileged people.

Two younger men joined with us in later years, Joe Ryan and Chuck Rosenow. Both were incisively intelligent, hard working and served with great distinction during both the Sedita and Makowski terms. Les Foschio, former Dean of Notre Dame's Law School, served as both Corporation Counsel and as Deputy Mayor, under Mayor Stanley Makowski, combining humanitarianism and keen legal intellect in the conduct of both offices.

And my new employment at City Hall gave me the opportunity to work with, to know, and to appreciate in a very special way, my father-in-law, Robert Moore. Bob, Notre Dame graduate and a Civil Engineer, was employed in Buffalo's Department of Urban Renewal. He had come to City Hall after completing a long and distinguished career at Great Lakes Dredge and Dock. He had served under two Commissioners of Urban Renewal, Jim Kavanaugh in the Kowal administration, and now under the direction of Dick Miller. Bob was highly esteemed in professional circles and was liked by all who met him. I had come into City Hall at a higher civil service level than Bob had attained, but he never displayed any animosity toward me, nor did he indicate in any way a suspicion that I had received my job as a political favor, or as a result of my friendship with Buz Roberts. After a few years, Bob paid me the professional compliment of asking, and respecting my opinions on job related matters. He accepted me as a 'professional peer', and our personal relationship, which was always strong, strengthened each year until his death at age 83.

I received my 'permanent' appointment as Project Manager after placing 1st in a NYS administered Civil Service Examination. Mayor Sedita had initially named me to an 'exempt' position in order to head the Allentown—Lakeview Concentrated Code Enforcement Project, but the housing inspectors union had brought suit claiming that only a 'qualified' housing expert could certify compliance with 'housing' regulations, and the City's Law Department ruled that a Civil Service examination had to be held in order to fill the 'title' of Project Manager. This was ironic because Buffalo businessmen and professionals, including myself and most of my associates, had traditionally held civil servants in low esteem, if not utter contempt. City and Erie County workers were generally viewed as shiftless, disinterested individuals who seldom earned their meager wages or exorbitant fringe benefits.

When I first began working at City Hall I was immediately struck with two overwhelming realities. The first, was that the working climate among a very large number of civil servants was far worse than I, or the general public, ever imagined. There seemed to be a general dedication to a work ethic that rewarded and reinforced indolence. The general consensus among the work force seemed to be that if one completed an assigned task, that they would then be given additional things to do,—and more than likely the new assignment would be more taxing or difficult to perform than the original assignment. So, one didn't "kill the job". Every simple assignment was made to last as long as possible. Civil service regulations didn't help either. While 'permanent' workers were protected from summary dismissal, or demotions, for political reasons, these same protective civil service regulations made it impossible for supervisors to weed out any but the most nefarious violators of good business practices and standards. Also, supervisors could not reward diligence, or even outstanding job performance, with extra pay or promotion to a higher position. All civil service promotions were based on a system of examination scores and pay raises were granted on the basis of seniority. Therefore, Civil Service regulations made it difficult to punish the indolent worker, and all but impossible to reward the industrious employee.

After only a few months 'on the job' the second reality became apparent to me. In his second term in office, Mayor Sedita had brought into City Hall a band of young, bright and personable men and women, who worked continuously and diligently to improve the lives of all Buffalonians. It must be recalled that in 1965, when Frank Sedita had sought the Democratic Party endorsement for Mayor, he had struck a deal with a young Joe Crangle, who was then attempting to solidify his position as the Democrat's Erie County Chairman. Under their agreement, Crangle was allowed to control the political patronage and financing and to wield complete political power and influence throughout New York State, so long as Frank Sedita was permitted to run City government unfettered and unrestricted by political considerations. Each man kept to the bargain throughout Sedita's final two terms as Mayor. Of course there were a few men appointed to positions in the City administration as a reward for political service, but even these few took their official duties seriously. I was unaware of any "no show" positions and the people that I worked with all seemed intent on not doing anything that would embarrass the Mayor, or discredit the Sedita Administration.

H. Buswell Roberts had been a Sedita confidant since Sedita had served as Erie County judge and now served as the Mayor's de facto 'chief of staff'. Anthony Manguso, Corporation Counsel and Dan Naples, Mayor's Secretary, were both boyhood chums of the Mayor. The three men demonstrated unbounded loyalty to Frank Sedita, at all times.

I was especially privileged in that each year that I worked in City government, I was engaged in conducting federal programs. Therefore, the City of Buffalo was fully compensated for every dollar that I earned as Project Manager, either from the Department of Housing and Urban Development (HUD), or later, from the Federal Emergency Management Agency (FEMA). This meant that, not only were my services costing Buffalo taxpayers nothing, but I, and the people under my supervision, were paid with federal dollars and were therefore subject to the provisions of the Hatch Act, which prohibit political activities by, or political interference with, civil servants on federal payrolls. Joe Crangle, somewhat reluctantly, acknowledged our unique position in City government and neither I, nor anyone else in the City's Department of Community Development was subject to any undue political pressures, insofar as I know.

It has been a source of personal pride that after four years, Allentown-Lakeview was successfully completed (more than 2500 residential structures were brought into compliance with the Buffalo Housing Code), on time, and under the budgeted amount. And, while we were meticulously and constantly scrutinized and audited, neither this, nor any other project that I headed over the years, was ever even slightly tainted by charges of corruption or scandal.

There were many neighborhood rehabilitation programs during the Sedita and Makowski terms. There were several reasons why Buffalo was selected to initiate so many New York State and Federal DHUD programs. Principally was the fact that Allentown-Lakeview CCE Project had been a success (a rare event in DHUD history) and that subsequent Buffalo programs had all been conducted free from scandal or corruption. Second, was the perception that grew in Washington, D.C. that "if a program can succeed in Buffalo, it can work anywhere."

This is not as negative as it seems. Buffalo's reputation for having horrendous weather was forever solidified by the 'Blizzard of '77." Buffalo's employment, income and other economic figures had been declining each year since the early 1950's (36,000 jobs had been lost in 1960 when Bell Aircraft moved to Texas). Buffalo's housing stock consisted of two-store wood framed dwellings, most of which were 100 years old. The U.S. Congress and the White House found Buffalo to be an excellent experimental laboratory for all sorts of social and community development programs.

As the years went by, and as Buffalo's real property tax base shrank, the only funds available for paving streets, replacing curbs, sidewalks and diseased trees, installing new street lights, refurbishing parks and playgrounds, or in general providing for the City's annual housekeeping needs, were those that were incorporated in the Neighborhood Rehabilitation Programs, which were all under my direction, and under the singular control of the Mayor.

This fact cemented Sedita's political strength. Any City department head, or any district councilman, who desired to get improvements made in any City neighborhood, had to come to me for the money. The Mayor decided where the federal and state funds could be put to the best use, thereby gaining the political kudos for making the improvements without special assessments or property tax increases. Where someone's request for street improvements, or a new park, had to be denied, the Mayor simply reported that it was Murphy's decision and that he had no control over the disbursement of federal funds. If a political leader wanted low income housing located in his district, the Mayor decided that it would be built. If a community resisted the imposition of low income housing into a middle-income neighborhood, the Mayor would disclaim all responsibility by stating that it was Murphy's responsibility to impose federal mandates and regulations and that there was nothing that the Mayor could do which would alter or countermand my actions. Sedita must have said to me a dozen times, "Murph, no one is ever going to vote for you!".

It was exhilarating to work in City Hall during this period, for in many ways these were among the most exciting and interesting years of our nation's and my city's history. While my assignments varied from month to month, and from year to year, and even though expressions of public approval and appreciation were rarely attained, I always felt that what I was doing was 'important'. I'd like to think that each day I gave my best effort toward improving living conditions for all Buffalonians. I'm only sure of the fact that I enjoyed making that effort.

In large measure, I was extremely fortunate to be forced to qualify for permanent civil service status, rather than serve in an exempt position and be beholden to a mayor, or a political party, for my continued public service. Not only was I freed from political pressures but almost simultaneous with my appointment to the City Hall position, on September 1,1967, the New York State Public Employees Fair Employment Act—The Taylor Law took effect,

—granting public employees the right to organize and to be represented by employee organizations of their own choice;

—requiring public employers to negotiate and enter into agreements with public employee organizations regarding their employees' terms and conditions of employment;

—establishing impasse procedures for resolution of collective bargaining disputes;

—defining and prohibiting improper practices by public employers and public employee organizations; and

—prohibiting strikes by public employees.

In other words, this Act made it possible for the wages and working conditions of public employees to become competitive with those existing in the private sector of the economy. Public servants soon began to receive salary increases every few years which quickly leveled the wage rates of public sector employees to those in the private sector. This 'leveling' of worker's compensation eventually eliminated the need for lower level civil servants to hold 'second front' jobs in order to make ends meet, and raised the public's expectation of 'quality' performance by public employees.

But neither the 'right to have a union' nor the higher salary levels of public workers stemmed the common perception that to get anything done at City Hall,—"palms had to be greased". I heard reports of 'under the table' payments in programs that I supervised, but I was never able to develop any kind of evidence of public employee, or contractor misbehavior. I never had any personal knowledge, but I also had no doubts, that policemen continued to 'flash the badge' to gain small favors in bars, restaurants, theaters and at sporting events, and that building inspectors might 'hold their hand out' in the hope of being rewarded for failing to notice minor infractions of the various municipal codes, even after public employee wages exceeded the subsistence level.

'Exempt' public employees and elected officials did not benefit overtly from the provisions of the Taylor Law, and there's absolutely no evidence that 'under the table' payments for political favors were diminished at all. But, I must state categorically that I never knew that any of my associates at City Hall had accepted any kind of gratuity, pay-off, or payment in return for a favor, or service rendered. I would be shocked today, if there were revelations of any corruption or collusion in the upper echelons of either the Sedita or Makowski City administrations.

As part of President Johnson's "war on poverty" the Economic Opportunity Act of 1964 created Community Action Organization (CAO), charged with providing community services, mobilizing public and private resources, and achieving "maximum feasible participation" of minority and low income residents. The Model Cities Program (1966) called on HUD to achieve widespread participation among those persons affected by its program grants. Then, the Housing and Community Development Act of 1974 merged Model Cities, urban renewal and other programs into a single Community Development Block Grant (CDBG) program. Cities applying for CDBG funds had to certify they had "provided adequate opportunity for citizen participation in the development of the applications for resident involvement in program activities."

If the purpose of this legislation and the ensuing regulations was to shift the responsibility for deciding how federal funds were to be spent, from the political parties (political bosses) to the private citizen, the aim was marginally achieved at best. The power of the political bosses to direct the expenditure of federal funds, was always extremely limited in Buffalo. But now the new legislation had fostered, and funded a host of fledgling organizations, each hoping to attract, and develop a constituency, by promising to obtain at least the 'fair share' of federal funds that was due to "the community". Each (CAO) organization used CDBG funds to hire "staff" in order to set and achieve their goals. Each (CAO) organization cajoled and pressured local politicians by promoting the CAO's ability to deliver, or withhold votes in the next election. The overall effect of all of this action, and activity, was not to directly increase the financial benefits directed to the average citizen, but rather to divert a considerable amount of federal dollars into the creation of an additional bureaucracy and to create a new (black) middle income class in Buffalo New York..

The National Environmental Policy Act (NEPA 1970) introduced environmental considerations into planning and instituted a process for evaluating the potential environmental, economic and other consequences of government action.

Public hearings, as well as approval of an 'Environmental Impact Statement', preceded the approval of any federally financed project. This had the effect of reversing the whole process of getting anything done at City Hall. Now, CAO agents were coming to the Hall to try to gain leverage in the decision making process and City workers were out in 'the community', attempting to inform, and be informed of, the most pressing needs of the citizens.

The work of City Hall professionals,—the urban planners, engineers, program designers, and architects, was not enhanced or diminished by the new regulations, or by the new body of overseers. A new form of 'democratic centralism' had been created. Public projects or works were simply delayed, and sometimes canceled, as a result of the protracted process of review, critique, oppose or approve, by 'community' groups. From my own personal knowledge I can think of several, innovative and beneficial projects, that withered and died during the application process, due to the insistence of 'community' representatives that the 'community', and not a city agency, be given the authority for management of minutia.

Many of the neighborhood rehabilitation projects were conducted concurrently. All of the projects contained a citizen participation component. There were usually several evening meetings held in various neighborhoods each week. I represented City Hall at almost all of these meetings. In the late 1960's and early 1970's, the assassinations of Martin Luther King, Robert Kennedy and Malcohm X had heightened racial tensions and a new mood of citizen activism produced many vitriolic confrontations at these neighborhood meetings.

It became common practice for me to join my colleagues for a drink or two at downtown bistros, after my attendance at these evening meetings. The usual outcome was that several times a week, I wouldn't get home until the wee hours of the morning. My marriage bonds, and the marital unions of my companions, were severely strained by these post work hours sessions. We earnestly believed that we were only extending the work day to a different location. But even though there was never any promiscuous or adulterous behavior, and City Hall business or politics were our usual topics of conversation (we seldom, if ever, discussed our family or private life), it was self-indulgent behavior and a childish waste of time, health and money.

And while I was running from meeting to meeting each day, and attending neighborhood meetings in the evening and then carousing into the early morning hours, there were responsibilities in the office, and at home, which demanded attention. I was blessed in several respects. During my first week in City Hall, Commissioner Miller assigned his department's best stenographer, Jan Purpura, to work in the Allentown-Lakeview Project. Jan was very attractive, demure, pleasant, and the most efficient administrative assistant I've ever witnessed. She quickly devised project record keeping and office procedures which I've since copied throughout my working years.

And at home, Barb continued to assume the full responsibilities of raising the family and maintaining the household. I found time to watch and to coach some Little League sports. I relished the hours that I spent coaching and scrimmaging with St. Marks basketball team. But, I took no part in the counseling and nurturing of my teenage daughters. Barb deserves full credit for (almost single-handedly) rearing eight children through the difficult teenage years to become the fine adults that they've each become. Even though the entire Murphy family has enjoyed 'good health', it hasn't always been easy. Both Barb and I suffered prolonged bouts of depression in our early 40's.

Barbara's outbreak was easy for me to understand. After 20 years of penury and hard labor, Barb felt herself abandoned, unwanted and abused. I was never around. The children were all in school and had their own circle of friends and activities. In the morning, when I had left for the office, and the children had trudged off, with their lunches and books in their backpacks, Barb was suddenly left alone in the house, with only the family dog, Ranger, to keep her company. And then,—Ranger scratched at the door, wanting to go outside. Sometimes it seems that life doesn't get much worse than that!

Barb slipped into a deep depressive state. She grew morose, lost her appetite and slept without resting. No gaiety, no argument or teasing, no supplication from friends or loved ones, could lift the veil of misery that had left Barbara bereft of self-esteem.

This condition persisted for several months, until one morning when I received a telephone call at the office telling me that Barb had a serious single car accident and had been taken to Sister's Hospital. I rushed to the hospital and found that Barb had miraculously escaped death, or even serious injury, when her auto had smashed head on into a large oak tree. When Barb returned home, after a brief stay in the hospital, her mood had brightened considerably. Once again, she began making plans and looking into the future, with the expectation of a pleasant and prolonged life.

Among the first of Barb's new announced ambitions, was a desire to seek employment outside the home. Shortly thereafter she passed a civil service exam and obtained a clerical position with Buffalo's Board of Education,—and she was on her way. After several promotions at the Board of Ed, and happy days spent with expanded friendships, Barb scored very high in a civil service exam for Court Clerk. She immediately received an appointment in the New York State Court System, where she was happily employed and served with great distinction until her retirement at the turn of the century. Barb never permitted her occupation to infringe upon her primary roles of wife, mother and grandmother. There was always time for me. No problem, or need for counseling, caring or assistance from the children or from the grandchildren, ever went unanswered. Barb succeeded in establishing her own identity and sense of self-worth, outside the constrictions of 'housekeeping'.

My period of depression was less pronounced, and less dramatic. A few years after Barb began her employment at the Board of Education, I began my slide into melancholia. I didn't know then, and I still don't understand today, what I thought was wrong in my life. I don't believe that I feared growing old. Barb's new employment had eliminated all strain on the family finances. I was unaware, and probably unconcerned about, the problems my teenager children were encountering entering the adult world. Anti-war and civil-rights protests left me unmoved. I was respected at work, I enjoyed the people that I worked with and I found my duties expansive, challenging and interesting. Yet I had entered a malaise, where I honestly thought that I didn't care whether I lived or died. I was in a humorless void, where I wasn't fit company for anyone. I met each attempt to cheer me with a shrug,—knowing that friends and loved ones didn't know what I was going through and didn't know what they were talking about either.

My escape from the morass is as puzzling and simplistic as my descent had been. While walking in a snowfall with Jim Burns, (we were returning from a Sabre's hockey game), I was moaning, moping and complaining about my lot in life. Suddenly Jim stopped short, turned to me and gruffly said,

> "Who the fuck ever told you that life was going to be great? Do you think that you're the only one who doesn't jump out of bed in the morning to say 'what a beautiful day this will be'?"

It doesn't seem profound now, but at that time I felt as if I had heard God's voice coming from a burning bush. I was over my depression! And, while at times since

I've felt myself on the brink of despair, I've always been able to pull back, remembering what an unbearable hell we can construct in our minds.

I don't know what causes depression. I don't know what cures depression. I only know that I never want to go there again!

Beginning in 1974, the Comprehensive Employment and Training Act (CETA) transformed the City Hall workplace by affording jobs and training to a whole new section of the population. No longer was employment in a government job solely dependent on one's ability to score well in Civil Service examinations, or performance for a political party or in a political campaign, or as a matter of birthright. The city government's work force was cleansed, invigorated, democratized and improved by the influx of new ethnics.

Shortly before the end of his third term Frank Sedita unexpectedly and without explanation, resigned the mayoralty and accepted the position of heading U.S. Customs in Western New York. The Common Council routinely appointed Stanley Makowski, the Deputy Mayor, to complete Sedita's term. Makowski then won re-election by a large margin and City Hall agendas continued unbroken and unchanged except for some minor changes in the Mayor's team.

Buz Roberts' steadying influence had been lost when he was elected Chief Judge of Buffalo's City Court. Frank Sedita's cronies, Dan Naples and Anthony Manguso, had retired when Sedita left office. Les Foschio, an extremely bright young man, succeeded Manguso as Corporation Counsel and John Downing, former Public Works Commissioner, now served as Deputy Mayor. The strengthened influence of Joe Crangle, Democratic Party Erie County Chairman, was also increasingly felt throughout City Hall.

There was also a stark difference in style. Sedita had routinely used the device employed by FDR of instigating discussion or argument from two opposing factions. The Mayor then sat back and enjoyed a rambunctious contest. At the conclusion of the fractious meeting Sedita would announce his decided course of action. Everyone present at the meeting would leave his office knowing what was to be done. There were never complaints, there were never hard feelings and there was never any indecision or reluctance on anyone's part to do the Mayor's bidding.

Stanley Makowski had served as a City Councilman for sixteen years before accepting the appointment as Deputy Mayor. His distinguishing trait, rare among politicians, was a genuine sense of humility. A veteran of World War II, Stan was a daily communicant, a dedicated family man, a man of high principles, with true compassion for the plight of the underprivileged.. He was truly "a man of the people." His years in the legislature had taught Stan to 'listen' in discussions, rather than debate or propose actions. He had learned to marshall his advocacy on any issue until he was sure that there was solid, majority support and then, and only then, did Makowski propose or support any action. We soon learned that, in contrast to the Sedita style of confrontation and immediate decision, Stan would meet with a succession of staff members and he would agree with each proposal. It soon became apparent to all of us that the last man to see the Mayor—won the argument! Stan Makowski was truly a 'good man'. He was a fine politician and legislative leader. In my opinion he was also a 'lousy' mayor, because in contrast to Sedita, Makowski didn't enjoy being mayor. He took no joy in the political infighting, nor in the office's pomp and ceremonies. He rarely attended social functions. He seemed uncomfortable in the presence of business leaders, federal or state officials, other mayors, and even reporters. But he was loved by the public, and was one of Buffalo's all-time best vote getters! Stan Makowski had no enemies!

Both the Sedita and Makowski administrations were staffed by energetic young men and women who had been infused by the words and ideals of Adlai Stevenson and John F Kennedy. It was my belief then, and remains my belief today, that each person that I worked with during those halcyon days, whether those persons be political friend or foe, sincerely felt that their efforts really mattered,—that "one man could make a difference" and that public service was a 'privilege and an honor'. I never knew of anyone in the top echelons of the Sedita/Machowski City administrations who took any action for "personal financial gain". No one viewed their position in City Hall as a stepping stone into the more lucrative 'private' sector, even though many of the professionals,—lawyers, engineers, architects and administrators, could command much higher fees from private employers. Even our political archenemy, Republican Councilwoman Alfreda Slominski, who held political and social beliefs diametrically opposed to those of myself and my associates, over time, won our respect with her dedication to professionalism and principles.

Several times I was the 'last one to see' Mayor Makowski and therefore was able to get my ideas implemented. While I was attending a federal conference in Boston, Mass., I visited Boston's Housing Court and spent some time with Boston's first Housing Court Judge. He explained the conditions that had prompted the

City of Boston to establish this innovative and independent means of settling landlord/tenant disputes, thereby putting some teeth into the enforcement of Boston's Housing Code. In many major aspects Boston's problems (and solutions) mirrored Buffalo's situations and conditions. When I returned to Buffalo I immediately enlisted the support of Chief Judge H.B. Roberts and we convinced the Mayor to create the Buffalo Housing Court. The new court was established and staffed within one month of my visit to Boston.

On another occasion I became aware, through NY Times articles, of a program that was being used to transform underutilized loft space in Manhattan into housing units for artists and middle income professions. The newspaper referenced the activity as 'the Section 235 program'. We did some research and discovered that Section 235 of the New York State Legislation permitted those cities who were subject to the N.Y.S. Multiple Dwelling Law to grant abatements of real property taxes under certain proscribed circumstances. New York City and Buffalo were the only cities in New York State to whom Section 235 applied! New York was using this exclusive privilege to convert underutilized commercial space into badly needed middle-income housing. We quickly drafted legislation that enabled Buffalo to provide relief of property taxes to developers who converted and rehabilitated commercial, industrial and public buildings into residential units. Within three weeks, the drafted legislation and regulations were endorsed by both daily newspapers, approved by the Buffalo Common Council, and signed into law by Mayor Makowski at 9:30 P.M., in his home, and on the last day permitted by the enabling New York State Legislation. This abatement program also provided the impetus for the creation of Buffalo's Theatre District Revitalization Program.

Buffalo's residential neighborhoods were plagued by deteriorating 100 year old, wooden frame homes. Old industrial and warehouse buildings, vacant and abandoned by their owners as not worth repairing or salvaging, dotted every section of the City. Eventually, the City obtained these wrecks under tax foreclosure proceedings. Unsalvageable buildings were demolished and structurally sound buildings were boarded up and secured against further vandalism or destruction. Yet, the unkempt vacant lots and boarded up buildings were themselves neighborhood blighting influences. NYS Municipal Law prohibited the City from acquiring, selling, or gifting real property except for "public purposes" or unless the property was included in an 'approved urban renewal (slum clearance) program'.

In order to provide the City with a means of transferring title to distressed buildings, or vacant lots, to new owners who were willing to improve, maintain, and develop the parcels, I came up with the idea of declaring the entire City of Buffalo a 'distressed' area negatively impacted by a preponderance of low-income residents, and therefore eligible for designation as an 'urban renewal area'. The Buffalo Urban Renewal Agency (BURA) adopted a resolution declaring the City "a distressed area" and New York State and DHUD approved the entire City of Buffalo being designated "an urban renewal area."

I immediately drafted the Buffalo City Wide Urban Renewal Program which enabled the City to conduct both the 'Scattered Site Housing Program' and the 'Buffalo Urban Homestead Program'. Later, during the Griffin administration, this law made it possible to conduct the award winning Pratt-Whitney Neighborhood Housing Program.

This city wide 'urban renewal' designation did prove troublesome when HUD threatened to withhold all CDBG funds from Buffalo if we failed to construct 87 units of low income housing in neighborhoods that were "not presently impacted by low-income families." HUD had recently imposed this severe penalty on Yonkers, NY when that distressed community had failed to satisfy a similar HUD demand. In order to obtain designation as an urban renewal area, Buffalo had certified that all of our neighborhoods were "impacted by low-income families" which compounded our problem in meeting the HUD dictate. I was assigned the task of finding 'unimpacted' sites for 87 new homes. I received warnings from several political figures that if I were to designate either Buffalo's South or Lovejoy districts as the site for 'assisted' housing units, that we would be faced with a taxpayer's revolt, or much worse. I solved this dilemma by locating an uncommitted parcel of land located within the Waterfront Redevelopment Area and convincing HUD that this area was "unimpacted' since we had relocated the residents years before! Buffalo had dodged the bullet. We continued to receive the federal funds that we had grown to rely on for daily municipal needs.

These were truly 'days of Camelot' for me. A time of civic turmoil, yet a time when anything 'good' seemed possible. A time when everyone in City Hall was laboring mightily to improve conditions for all Buffalonians. One example of my personal euphoria was my singular adventure into the realm of City Hall politics.

The Buffalo Sewer Authority had wrestled with internal political turmoil for a number of years. With the construction of a new sewage treatment plant the

Authority had the opportunity to appoint a Superintendent of Sewage Treatment, a position that paid a very generous salary. Pressure from the local media against 'patronage' appointments forced the Authority to announce that the new position would be 'civil service' and that the new appointment would be made only after a New York State administrated civil service examination was held. As a lark, I signed up to take the exam. I took a few books from the Erie County Public Library in order to familiarize myself with terms like 'effluent', 'effluvium' and 'sludge'. On the day of the exam I was surprised to find that more than a dozen applicants had been deemed qualified to take this examination. The City's Commissioner of Public Works and two other City engineers were among the few men that I recognized. who were taking the test. After only a few weeks the results of the examination were announced. Only two applicants had received passing grades and I had attained the highest score of all applicants for the position!

The Civil Service Commission announced that since there were less than three names on the 'qualified' list of applicants, there was no requirement that the Sewer Authority choose their appointee from the civil service 'list'. Almost immediately the Sewer Authority appointed a crony of Joe Crangle, Erie County Democratic Chairman, to this high administrative office. Both Buffalo newspapers printed lead editorials condemning the Sewer Authority action and demanding that I be given the opportunity of filling the new position. But it was only so much 'baying at the moon' for the appointment was a 'fait accompli'. The most humorous aspect of the whole episode was the fact that only I knew that if the Sewer Authority had interviewed me for the job, they would have instantly discovered that I barely knew how to flush a toilet, much less run a sewage treatment plant!

It was also a time of personal contemplation and gradual awareness of personal change. After almost fifty years of being a 'practicing Catholic' I admitted to myself that I didn't believe in an Almighty God, nor did I believe in heaven or hell, nor in the infallibility of the Pope or many Catholic Church teachings and practices. I valued the virtues expressed in the Ten Commandments and I tried to adhere to the teachings of Jesus Christ. As I feared "the loss of heaven and the pains of hell" less, I came to love and to respect mankind, and all living things, more. I would like to think that since the day that I 'lost the Faith', I've become a better Christian. I know that I've tried not to harm anyone, in anyway, since that time. Leszek Kolakowski, Polish writer and philosopher, who describes his thinking as "humanist socialism", has written, "I am my brother's keeper, and as such, I have no right to tell him that there is no God". I also try to follow this dictate.

It was also the time that I felt the first pangs of dissatisfaction. I remember distinctly that on the day that our first born, Tommy, left the family nest, as he was backing out of the driveway, on his way to beginning a new life in California, family members were tearfully waving goodbye, and I thought, "Why am I not going to California? Why doesn't Tommy stay here and assume the responsibilities that I've shouldered for 25 years? I'm the one who has earned the right to get away from it all." There was no rancor in my mind, nor in my heart. Yet, on that day, I wasn't proud of that thought. I'm not proud of having had that thought today. But that's what I said to myself!

During the twelve years of the Sedita and Makowski municipal administrations, the nation experienced social and political malaise as it witnessed the assassination of many of it's young leaders, the conduct and inglorious conclusion of an unpopular war, racial and civil unrest in the cities and on the college campuses, misconduct in the highest office in the nation, an energy crisis and stagflation that threatened the fiscal strength of the country, and the creation of a counter-culture among the youth that emphasized drug use, free love, and loss of respect for all authority.

But, as former Speaker of the House Tip O'Neill often remarked, "All politics is local" and the overriding issue in Buffalo each and every year that I was in City Hall was the City's loss of "working' population and the shrinking revenue obtained from property taxes, which was the City's principal income source. Street crime was kept under control. Rioting and civil unrest never visited our streets. Forced 'busing' of school children in order to effect racial desegregation of the public schools, was met by vociferous opposition, but was managed without incident or physical violence. Student protest demonstrations on UB's campus were kept orderly by the actions of Buffalo's police. Religious leaders kept (nationally sponsored) boycotting and demonstrating at local abortion clinics reasonably peaceful through their example of restraint and urging from the local pulpits. But each succeeding census confirmed what was obvious to even a casual observer. Buffalo's population was shrinking each year, and the residents who remained were older, blacker and poorer than the multitudes who fled to the suburbs, or to warmer climes.

Buffalo real estate values continued to decline and the number of taxable properties shrunk to less than 50% of the land within the constricted City borders.
There was never a fiscal year that didn't begin with threats of employee layoffs,
incentives for early retirements, and proposals to trim or eliminate municipal services. The City of Buffalo had become a 'ward of the state', dependent upon New
York State and the federal government for the funds with which to maintain the
municipal parkland, infrastructure and affordable housing resources.

There was also the reality that economic conditions throughout Western New
York worsened during the Makowski term. In 1977, Bethlehem Steel announced
that it was closing it's steelmaking plant in Lackawanna, adding almost 20,000
workers to the unemployment rolls. Inclement weather (record Dec '76 snowfall,
Blizzard of '77 and the Ice Storm of 1978), proved disastrous to a city budget
already strained to the breaking point by the economic slowdown and plunging
real property values and tax receipts. At the end of his first full term as Buffalo
Mayor, Stan Makowski announced that he would not seek re-election, even
though all political polling showed that he was an unbeatable candidate. Les Foschio, Buffalo's Corporation Counsel, and an extremely bright and creative man,
received the Democratic Party endorsement in the 1977 mayoral primary contest.

NYS Assemblyman Arthur Eve, longtime Black activist, immediately announced
his intention of opposing Foschio in the race for the Democratic mayoral nomi-
nation. NYS Senator Jimmy Griffin, maverick Democrat, first obtained the
endorsement as the Conservative Party mayoral candidate and then announced
that he would contest in the Democratic Party Primary elections as well.

I financially supported and personally worked hard in behalf of Les Foschio in
the Democratic Primary activities. When the votes were counted, Foschio and
Griffin had split the white votes, and Art Eve had received solid support from the
black community. Eve became the Democratic nominee for Mayor.

Jimmy Griffin was the Conservative Party candidate, and the Republicans put
forth John Phelan, who had never held elective office, as their candidate. I knew
all three men, and I had worked with Eve and Phelan in past government activities. But I didn't work for, or support in any fashion, the political efforts of any of
the candidates in the general election.

In November 1977, Conservative Party Candidate, Jimmy Griffin, was elected Buffalo's Mayor.

In Ireland, "the slurry season" is that time of the year before planting, when farmers spread a watery mixture of cow manure over their fields, producing a stench that hovers over the countryside. In my opinion, Griffin's tenure as Buffalo's mayor produced a 'slurry season' in City Hall that lasted for sixteen years.

Griffin is my first cousin, although I only casually knew him, as either child or adult, until he became Buffalo's Mayor. There was no hostility or acrimony between us. We simply had never before traveled in the same social or political circles. Mayor Makowski knew of this familial relationship, and in recognition of that fact and because my civil service status would insure my continued employment in City Hall following Griffin's election, he appointed me to direct the transition to the incoming Griffin administration.

In 1978 Jimmy Griffin became Buffalo's mayor. Griffin, a maverick Democrat who had waged a war against Erie County's Democratic headquarters for decades, brought a whole new cast of characters, and a completely different attitude toward public service, into City Hall. Many of the new administrators were extremely capable, honest and energetic, but some were not. All were dedicated to the propositions that whatever had been tried by past City administrations had been misguided effort, and that whatever had been previously accomplished, had been achieved by corruption. Griffin had been elected on the Conservative Party ticket, and he therefore felt that he wasn't beholden to any political party or organization. He retained a long "enemy list" and his minions were relentless and ruthless in ferreting out political party stalwarts, suspected dissidents and other potential critics, discharging those without civil service protection and making continued public service so unbearable for the rest, that they resigned or retired from public employment. A few of Griffin's subordinates were convicted of hoodlumish labor practices and served jail terms.

Griffin had brought with him some extremely capable administrators and public servants. Joe Martin, Griffin's aide-de-camp in Albany, Ronald Anthony, IBM executive and Stan Buczowski, City Councilman, in particular displayed pragmatic zeal in effecting change and in the elimination of what they considered to be waste and corruption. It soon became evident that the pervasive mood was that anything attempted in the Sedita/Makowski period was considered ill-conceived. Any program or activity initiated in the Makowski term was allowed to wither. Erie County Executive Ned Regan, a Republican, welcomed Griffin as an ally and gleefully offered the new mayor a few experienced public administrators to assist in continuing community development efforts. Larry Quinn was appointed Economic Development Coordinator and William Donahue was named Commissioner of Community Development by Griffin. They immediately adopted two Makowski administration initiatives, Theatre District Restoration and American Cities consultant contract for Downtown Redevelopment, as their own concepts. Mayor Griffin joined with County Executive Regan in cutting ribbons at the newly constructed Convention Center and at the Erie Basin Marina.

During the first weeks of the new Griffin administration, Dan Walkowiak, Buffalo Urban Renewal Agency (BURA) counsel and I were instructed to bring the newly appointed City department heads and members of the BURA up to date on ongoing projects and activities. Walkowiak, who had dedicated 15 years to ferreting through a maze of New York State and Federal HUD regulations, instructions, and restrictions, explained to the new staff the obstacles that made getting anything accomplished difficult, the legal avenues available to circumventing these obstacles, as well as the heavy penalties that could be incurred if federal or state laws were ignored or flaunted. Walkowiak was dismissed as BURA counsel two days after his briefings ended.

I was invited to address the members of the Buffalo Urban Renewal Agency at their first meeting with Mayor Griffin as chairman. I described the projects and programs in progress, their objectives and scheduled activities. I described the programs for which the City had already obtained federal approvals, their objectives and the proposed schedule of implementation. Finally, I outlined the applications for federal/state funds that had been submitted but that had not yet been approved. At the conclusion of the meeting all of the BURA members expressed their appreciation to me for the inclusive and informative briefing. I met privately with a fuming Mayor Griffin a few moments later. He harshly said to me, "I don't want them told all those details. You tell me and I'll tell them (BURA members) what I want them to know!"

I was dumbfounded! I had no way of knowing then that Griffin was going to ignore, deny, and obliterate the commitments and planning of the previous municipal administrations. He was determined to do things his way! And if his way wasn't the correct way, it at least would be different than what his predecessors had wanted. I also had never expected that, like Walkowiak, I would be excluded from all future BURA actions and decisions. I wasn't invited to attend any additional BURA meetings during Mayor Griffin's tenure. From that day forward, I only received mayoral assignments that were in no way related to housing or to community development.

A radical change took place in the ways that federal funds were directed and used during the Ronald Reagan presidency. No longer were federal dollars to be used "to encourage the creation of housing development and service organizations designed to focus on the housing needs of low-income families and individuals", as required by the Economic Opportunity Act of 1964. Using the newly created Urban Development Action Grants, the Griffin Administration was able to steer the loan of federal dollars to Goldome Bank, Shea's Buffalo Theater, General Cinema Corporation, Hyatt Hotels and several local businessmen. Few of the loans were fully repaid. Federal dollars were diverted from affordable housing and neighborhood revitalization projects to construct a new baseball stadium in downtown Buffalo and luxury housing units on Buffalo's waterfront. A few top officials in the Griffin administration voluntarily left municipal service to go to work for local banks, national developers (who obtained government financing for Buffalo developments) or to manage local construction activities. There was never any accusations of 'conflict of interest', nor was any Griffin associate ever charged with misappropriating government funds, so that we must assume that all of the expenditures of public funds met "the letter of the law".

Over the years I made three proposals to the Griffin administration for the use of CDBG funds. First, I proposed that the Rapid Transit Corridor (one block on each side of Main Street) be designated for CDBG financed redevelopment; second, I proposed that CDBG funds be used to establish a 'credit union' in the inner city which would provide financing to the black community for private redevelopment; and lastly, I proposed that CDBG funds be used to build and equip a manufactured homes plant and that CETA funds be used to hire and train the inner-city residents who would eventually manage and staff the manufacturing facility. None of my proposals received even cursory consideration by the Griffin Community Development staff.

There is one facet of the Makowski administration that was continued and expanded for which I share at least partial credit or shame. In the latter years of the Makowski administration, City budgetary constraints forced mandatory retirements, as well as early retirement inducements, in order to lower City payroll expenses. In the Department of Community Development, a few professional and technical personnel had been removed from the City's payroll (civil service) and placed on a newly created BURA staff chart (which was 100% funded by federal HUD dollars).

During the 'transition' discussions, Griffin was emphatic that he wanted BURA, and in particular the BURA staff, abolished. I explained the legal and fiducial benefits to the Mayor of retaining the Buffalo Urban Renewal Agency and I emphasized that while it was easy for the Mayor to fire BURA personnel (they had no civil service or union protection), destroying the staffing structure might prohibit Griffin from making pragmatic moves at some future date. After some deliberation, and I'm sure after consultations with other advisors, Griffin decided to retain the Buffalo Urban Renewal Agency as the principal administrative body for federal HUD funds. Griffin did fire the BURA staff, but he retained the staff structure. Soon after he became Mayor, several City employees were offered promotions, raises, or were simply instructed to apply for BURA positions and to forsake the salary structures and civil service protection of City of Buffalo employment. Soon, City budgets showed marked reductions in the payrolls of Community Development, Parks, and Public Works departments, as jobs were shifted over to the federally funded BURA staff payroll. Eventually almost the entire Department of Community Development consisted of BURA staff, answerable only to the Mayor,—not to the Common Council, and certainly not to the City Comptroller. These shifts didn't reduce payroll expenditures. Nor were City taxpayers provided one nickel of tax relief, but it appeared to the citizenry that Jimmy Griffin had succeeded in cleaning out the wasteful expenditures that he had railed against during the election campaign.

In fact, transferred employees were not restricted by union pay scales or civil service test scores. Nor were they protected by seniority rights or civil service tenure. Many political scores were settled as real and imagined affronts to the Griffin persona were settled by summary dismissal from BURA employment. Power politics had returned to City Hall and neither Civil Service status, nor the protection of the Democratic (or Republican) political machine, could save those who came into Jimmy Griffin's disfavor.

After the Blizzard of '77 devastated the community and city services, the City of Buffalo received financial assistance from a number of federal sources. The Mayor's Office had received $25,000 FEMA grant to prepare a Snow Emergency Response Program. Mayor Griffin asked me to administer the FEMA grant. I designed a plan to use existing NFTA equipment and facilities, to evacuate the

Downtown Business District, in the event that another calamity occurred during the business work week. In cooperation with the Buffalo Board of Education and the American Red Cross, I established a series of emergency shelters in the public high schools, which were located in all sections of the City. Additionally, I designed a program which coordinated the personnel, equipment and activities of all City departments for emergency operations in the event of any kind of catastrophe.

But my personal coup was the discovery that Erie County was no longer a designated 'civil defense' community and received no FEMA funds, due to the County's failure to maintain a Civil Defense office and staff. In the Buffalo Snow Emergency Response Program, I included an entire cadre of 'Civil Defense' staff positions, who would plan, execute, and administer all future City of Buffalo Emergency Response activities. I then submitted an application to FEMA, requesting that the City of Buffalo be designated a 'Civil Defense' Community and requested that FEMA reimburse the City for the salaries and attendant expenses of the Civil Defense staff. The City received almost immediate approval of both requests and I designated existing City personnel, (fire and police department staff principally) to 'Civil Defense' positions. In this manner, the City of Buffalo received FEMA reimbursement for more than $300,000 payroll each year, without adding a single person to the City's personnel roster.

For the next six years, I completed monthly Civil Defense reports and annual budgets; I prepared and received Civil Defense approvals for, six additional 'Emergency Response' program, (i.e.) Toxic Chemical Spills, Flooding, Nuclear Reactor Accident, etc., I attended monthly meetings with other CD personnel (from Jamestown, Batavia, Lockport, Niagara Falls, etc). I attended the FEMA Emergency Response seminars and classes in Gettysburg PA and I was in constant contact with Toronto, Ontario Emergency Response staff, who had recently conducted an evacuation of a small city (250,000 pop.) after a propane and other chemical spill, and who had contributed greatly to relieving the overworked Buffalo crews and equipment during the Blizzard of '77. My work was the sole justification for FEMA sending Buffalo $300,000 each year.

FEMA had sent a copy of the City of Buffalo Snow Emergency Response Program to the U.S. Conference of Mayors, as an example of the type of emergency planning that was being undertaken by enlightened U.S. municipalities. As a result of this submission I was designated as the U.S. Conference of Mayors' representative on the FEMA National Policy Advisory Committee. As such, I appeared before FEMA boards and worked with FEMA staff in Washington, D.C. on several occasions.

None of this is meant to imply that I was a key member of Mayor Griffin's staff, or even a cog in the Griffin administration machine. I really don't know how much the Mayor knew about what I was doing. I know that I didn't report my activities to him, or to anyone else, on a regular basis. I know that I was told that I was not welcome at the weekly meetings that Griffin conducted with his department heads. I was also warned that my tendency to present another 'point of view' during policy discussions was viewed as 'negativism' by Griffin and his displeasure had been adopted by his closest associates. It was reported to me that many City Hall eyes viewed me as an enemy of the Griffin administration.

In all fairness to Jimmy Griffin, I was extremely uncomfortable with the constant criticism of past City administration efforts and intentions. One of the requirements of the City's 'Civil Defense' agreement with FEMA, was that a 'command post' be created from which emergency response directions could be given in the event of a calamity or crisis situation. I saw an opportunity to establish a personal hermitage. I had my telephone extension, a desk, files and an air conditioner installed in windowless space in City Hall's sub-basement and I notified FEMA that we had established an emergency command post. I remained readily accessible by telephone but I was also 'out of sight'. I never told Griffin of this 'secret' office, although I spent a considerable amount of my City Hall time there. Eventually, I got the report that the Mayor's confidants reported that I was using City Hall's back stairwell to escape City Hall during the workday.

During this same period of time, Griffin had also assigned me the duties of Energy Conservation Coordinator. As such I conducted energy audits of municipal buildings and facilities, and promulgated rules for the conservation of fuel and energy in City vehicles and buildings. I also ordered a study of the viability of using 'wind power' to provide electricity to the Buffalo Naval Park and to Buffalo's Memorial Auditorium. Finally, I conducted several meetings with local utility company executives in order to investigate the feasibility of creating a 'central heating district' in downtown Buffalo and in using the (under construction) underground rapid transit tunnels as conduits for heat and utilities to four hospitals along the rapid transit corridor. Then I was asked to supervise a consultant's study on the feasibility of creating a municipally owned power company (replacing Niagara Mohawk).

While many of my assigned and assumed tasks were interesting to me, and several seemed important for the City's well-being, the simple truth is that no one in the Griffin administration cared about what I was doing, or what I thought. I was representing the City of Buffalo, and speaking in behalf of the Mayor, throughout Erie County, throughout New York State and in Washington, D.C., yet I had little contact with the Mayor, and I had no confidence that if I mis-spoke, or overstated a municipal position, that I would receive any support from the Griffin administration.

It became painfully apparent to me that my days as an influential City Hall insider were over. I enrolled at SUNYAB in their Masters of Urban Planning Program and began taking classes. The faculty at SUNYAB, particularly Dr. Harold Cohen, Dean of SUNYAB's School of Architecture, were extremely cooperative. I was granted no special privileges, except that class schedules were designed to accommodate my work schedule. During 20 years of civil service, I had accumulated a considerable amount of unused vacation and compensatory time. By judiciously using this accumulated time off, one half-day at a time, and using the seclusion of the Civil Defense command center for privacy and study, I was able to satisfactorily complete 62 hours of graduate studies in three years time. I was awarded a Masters degree in Urban Planning (MUP) in August 1983. All the while, I singularly met all the responsibilities of both Director of Emergency Services and Director of Energy Conservation with distinction.

Originally, my enrollment in graduate studies was a lark, an exercise in egotism. I didn't see any way in which an advanced degree would earn me more money, gain me prestige, or open future political or governmental opportunities. But after I had successfully completed several courses and had become familiar with several stimulating faculty members, I began to fantasize that I might be able to assume a faculty position at SUNYAB, after I took early retirement from the City of Buffalo at my age of 55. All that was needed was twelve additional hours of graduate credit, which would be spent in preparing my PHD dissertation.

This fantasy crashed on the day that I received my Master's Degree diploma. A Buffalo News reporter told me that the City of Buffalo 1984 budget provided for only one job being eliminated. That job was Project Manager! My civil service position was being terminated! I immediately telephoned Mayor Griffin, who brusquely said, "you're going to have to take less money next year." When I asked the reason for this decision, the Mayor announced, "I don't want to talk about it!" Then, he hung up on me. The Commissioner of Administration and Finance refused to see me or to take my calls. No member of the Griffin administration would ever give me a reason for my dismissal!

I sent Mayor Griffin a letter resigning my position as Director of Civil Defense, but urged that the 'Civil Defense' (Emergency Management) staff and functions be continued, as a display of fiscal prudence and civic responsibility. My letter was never acknowledged in any way.

The next day, I reported to the Department of Community Development and informed Commissioner Quinn that Civil Service regulations stated that when a position is eliminated, a tenured employee had a right to 'bump' a less seasoned employee from a similar title at the same grade, or if that was impossible, that the tenured staff member had a right to a position for which he was qualified, beneath the eliminated position. I requested appointment to the position of Assistant Project Manager, which was included in the 1984 City Budget projection. Quinn quickly eliminated the Civil Service title of 'Assistant Project Manager' from the new budget and I was forced to accept the position of 'Project Coordinator' which was four pay grades ($7,000) below what I had been earning.

On my 52nd birthday, after seventeen years of dedicated and effective public service, under the direction of three mayors, and with my brand new Masters Degree in hand, I found myself,—a pariah in City Hall, powerless, friendless and three years short of being able to apply for 'early retirement'. I had been on the sidelines and watched as a good friend, Bob Bradley had acquired health care facilities, office buildings and hotels and had amassed a private fortune by providing skillful management to distressed realty. I saw another friend, Phil Schwab, attain dizzying financial success in the construction business, only to be brought crashing down through a series of innuendo, false charges and legal maneuvering. I witnessed my former employer, Ed Cottrell, make a mockery of Erie County government as he looted millions from the public coffers with the simple promise to build a 'domed' stadium. I hadn't made a nickle, or profited in any way, from any of these schemes or actions.

5

APPROACHING RETIREMENT

"To know how to grow old is the masterwork of wisdom, and one of the most difficult chapters in the great art of living."

—**Henri-Frederic Amiel,**
Swiss philosopher

My plight was hardly pitiable. The entire family was enjoying excellent health. Barb was firmly established in a stimulating work environment and was radiant with the knowledge of her self-worth. We were not yet 'empty nesters', but several of the children had mated or had established their own residences. The younger members of the family were still in school, but each child had financed their own college costs, so that the family coffers were not besieged by extraordinary expenses. I had long since ceased my late night carousing and I hadn't taken a drink at lunchtime since Jimmy Griffin's inauguration. Barb and I were active, playing tennis together and with other partners. We finally had the time and resources with which to travel. We paid regular visits to Cape Cod to visit with Barb's sister, Molly. We took a trip to Ireland and used our time-sharing program to explore warm climes for winter, retirement residences. I resumed playing golf, but I could never feel any passion, or even affection for the game. Golf was, and still is, a somewhat pleasant way to kill off a few hours.

Most importantly, our marriage was solid as a rock. Over the years, I had observed any number of marriages and romances wither and die from over familiarity and boredom. Other marital unions had exploded over unrealized expectations, or financial stress, or by libidinous pursuits. Most commonly, I saw good friends and lovers pull gradually apart as their intellectual or emotional needs outpaced their mate's capacities. I have always been amazed, and awed by the fact that Barbara and I grew in love and respect for each other, every month of our married life. There was always mutual trust and our confidence that we could weather any adversity, if we faced it together.

Even my situation at City Hall was hardly precarious. I had never depended upon familial relations to protect me from Jimmy Griffin's irascible temperament. I was the only member of the Sedita/Makowski administrations that was protected by civil service status against summary dismissal or demotion. I hadn't taken any action, nor publically expressed any opinion, that warranted political or personal reprisal.

Nor would I never relinquish the shield that civil service status provided me for I knew that Larry Quinn, Commissioner of Community Development, was my enemy. Quinn seemed to resent what he felt was my latent influence on Mayor Griffin, and I think that he feared that I might disrupt his collegial relationship with Goldome Bank and thwart their pending Theater District development schemes. But, I also thought that I knew the rules of governance as well as any member of the Griffin administration, and I was confident that I could survive any political in-fighting instigated by Larry Quinn.

After retrospection, I probably should have pursued the PhD degree in Public Administration and attempted to obtain a faculty position at SUNYAB or at another NY State institution. Failing that, I could have settled back and rode out the professional discourtesy and debasement that was to come. But my old enemy, "Vanity," struck at me again. I wasn't old, in body or spirit, and I wanted to prove, maybe only to myself, that I was still as good as I always thought I was. I began by investigating scores of 'get rich' quick, (private sector) schemes. I obtained a real estate broker's license and made a half-hearted, part-time attempt at realty sales. I investigated purchasing a couple of businesses (an employment agency and a bookstore).

Finally, I bought into a program that I saw advertised somewhere, after only a cursory examination. I paid $7,500 to attend a three-day seminar in Chicago, that promised instruction and administrative support in the field of purchasing real property from financially distressed owners, before foreclosure action by a lending institution, and the resale of the property at a substantial profit. The beauty of the scheme was that the basic tools necessary for success were diligence and industry. It was after only a few hours at the seminar that I knew that I had been conned. I had spent $7,500 to obtain instruction on how to take advantage of people when they were most vulnerable and to convert their financial and personal chaos into a quick profit for me. The principal irony was the fact that the scheme seemed most viable in a city with pockets of economic distress (unemployment), but with escalating real property values. This was definitely not the situation in Buffalo, N.Y.!

But "vanity" isn't defeated so easily. I was determined that I wouldn't return from the seminar and admit that I had thrown $7,500 down a sewer. I told Barb that this was a viable business scheme and that I thought that I had found an income niche and respectable occupation that could be pursued in any part of the nation during our retirement years. In my heart I hoped to recoup my initial investment, using my industry alone and without making any further substantial outlay of capital, and without hurting any homeowner, who was suffering financial distress.

I established "Crescent Mortgage Corporation" and spent my leisure time during the next few years tracking homeowners who were hopelessly delinquent in their mortgage payments, appraising the value of the mortgaged property, and attempting to calculate a quick resale selling price. Even in the declining Buffalo market I was able to find a few opportunities. The first homeowner that I contacted turned out to be a young businessman, who had overextended his credit with the gambling community, and had not informed his wife that they were about to lose their home through bank foreclosure proceedings. I walked away from that business opportunity, without further word and with no regrets.

Later I found a family in Hamburg NY, the husband had been laid off by Bethlehem Steel Company but he was expecting a 'recall'. This decent family was desperate to preserve their 'credit' status and to continue to live in their cherished home. They perceived that their only hope of preserving their dignity was to avert bank foreclosure by signing over their ownership rights to Crescent Mortgage Corp. I feared that neither I, nor the homeowners, had the resources to weather the Bethlehem Steel Plant closing and I backed out of an agreement to buy, then lease back, the Hamburg NY home to the previous owners.

There was also a dilapidated chalet, along with more than forty acres of wooded land in Holland, NY, where the owner's attorney kept insisting that I had made an offer to assume the defaulted mortgage and that his client had accepted my offer. In this instance I refused to consummate the acquisition because I feared the nature and extent of needed repairs. More importantly, I knew nothing about assessing the value of rural property.

I just couldn't bring myself to take advantage of the misfortunes of others. I was also extremely reluctant to risk more of my lifetime savings solely in order to make more money. I passed on these three, and all other opportunities to purchase about-to-be foreclosed properties

Crescent Mortgage Corporation eventually purchased five apartments on Buffalo's West Side for $42,000. I made some repairs and modernized the plumbing and electrical services and I placed the units in HUD's Section 8 Housing Program. Here I was, back in my principal field—low-income housing. But this time as a landlord not as a program administrator. I was determined to provide decent housing to those who needed it, and to earn a reasonable rate of return on my investment of time and money. What I received was an education in socio-economics and socio-cultural behavior that will be forever etched in my psyche.

Among my lessons learned:

—the number and nature of things that can go wrong in a 100 year old wooden structure is inexhaustible;

—a deteriorating neighborhood makes it difficult to attract respectable tenants, or to retain stable family units, even if the rental units are well-maintained;

—tenants who have all utilities included in their rent, can, and will quickly exhaust a landlord's monetary and emotional reserves;

—poor people will commit despicable actions, if they're given no alternative;—there are people who do evil, not because they're rich or poor, not because they're ignorant, but because they are evil;

—the oppression of poverty upon the poor, worsens the poverty, and the poorer the family (or person), the worse is the oppression. (<u>No one is willingly poor!</u>)

—Erie County's Department of Social Services (and some 'charitable' organizations) seldom benefit their clients. They provide an endless string of obstacles between the 'needy' and any remedial action or benefit. They have no interest in pursuing 'welfare cheats' or detecting or preventing criminal activity. They view all inquiries, suggestions, or criticisms from the (unassisted) 'public' as intrusive.

I really worked hard over the next eight years to make the West Side properties a viable investment. Invaluable assistance was provided me by a contractor, Sal Morreale, who was as hard working and honest as any contractor I ever came into contact with. But every small step of progress was met by further slippage into a financial abyss:

—an undetected, malfunctioning city water meter cost several thousand dollars in delinquent charges;

—three evictions, after prolonged nonpayment of rent, resulted in the apartment being completely trashed by tenants, before their departure;

—irresponsible, and sometimes hostile tenant actions resulted in horrendous utility expenses;

—the changing ethnicity of the neighborhood prolonged each vacancy period.

After years of toil, and frustration and penury, I surrendered. Crescent Mortgage Corporation deeded ownership of the property to Sal Morreale. Sal assumed the future mortgage payments, but no additional recompense was received by Crescent Mortgage Corp. A few years later, I closed out Crescent Mortgage Corporation as a legal entity.

There is irony here, and a lesson to be learned. The irony is that Crescent Mortgage was formed to protect me and my assets from legal or financial penalties from realty transactions and operations. Crescent Mortgage Corporation lost money every year of its operation,—not paper losses, real money! Yet I couldn't deduct any of the expenses for searching for foreclosure properties, nor the apartment utility charges, nor the expensive repairs to vandalized apartments, from my personal income. These tax deductions had to be charged each year to Crescent Mortgage Corporation: which never earned a profit or owed even a penny in federal income tax. New York State Corporations are subject to a minimum state income tax, which was not reduced by deductions and had to be paid each year regardless of the annual monetary loss.

The lesson to be learned—it's easy to fool yourself!

The singular benefit of my landlord experience was the relief it afforded me from the tedium at City Hall. When I reported for assignment as 'Project Coordinator' at the Department of Community Development, I was given the most mundane tasks. Two separate supervisors, at two separate intervals, told me that Commissioner Quinn had directed that I not be given office space, but that my desk should be placed in a public corridor as a display of chastisement. Both women told me that they refused the Commissioner's order. Both women were subsequently dismissed from their City Hall positions, but months after the mentioned insubordinations. Meanwhile, each time that I left City Hall premises to inspect dilapidated structures prior to demolition orders, I was followed in an attempt to find me in 'dereliction of duty'. Finally, I was assigned a single duty which prohibited my leaving City Hall during working hours. I was assigned the task of monitoring the use of a set of filing cabinets, and I was specifically, and singularly, excluded from staff meetings. Further, I was told by people that I trusted, that the 'word' was out that I would be dismissed from City service before I reached the normal retirement age of 62.

Throughout these ordeals I attempted to adopt the attitudes of "Cool Hand Luke,"—the more menial the task,—the more cheerful my attitude became and I vowed to myself that I would perform the most servile task better than it had ever been done before!

This continued for more than two years, until Jim Comerford, Commissioner of Public Works, asked me if I would object to being assigned as a 'loaned executive' to Buffalo's United Way campaign. Comerford explained that I would remain on the City payroll, but that I would receive my work assignments from the United Way staff for the duration of their annual fund-raising campaign (about three months). He said to me, "I thought that you could use some relief from the hell you're being put through." I thanked him and reported to the 1988 United Way Campaign in August of that year. My daily assignments were to visit workplaces and to address the employees there, describing the values to the local community provided by United Way, and asking the workers to pledge to contribute a small stipend from each paycheck during the coming year. I enjoyed every hour of my United Way assignments.

However, on my 56th birthday, my father died. Dad had suffered a stroke some eight years previous and he had spent the final four years of his life in a nursing home, unable to communicate or care for himself in anyway. After years of confinement, and helplessness, Dad eventually lost his desire to live. I was never close to my father, and as I became an adult we drew even further apart. To my shame, I seldom visited Dad during his years of nursing home confinement. I was afraid to admit, even to myself, that the sight of this feeble old man,—who was only twenty-four years older than I,—terrified me!

After the funeral, and helping to arrange Dad's affairs, I returned to my United Way assignment. But six weeks after my father's death, Mom was found dead on the floor of my sister Pat's home, where Mom had been living. Pat had been most attentive to my father during his senior years and during his nursing home confinement. Similarly, Pat was the one that Mom relied on for all of life's necessities,—food, shelter, transportation, and conversation, after Dad's impairment.

Late in my mother's life our relationship had been strained by a peculiar phenomenon,—her nephew, Jimmy Griffin, had been elected Mayor of Buffalo! And, while she never knew Jimmy Griffin well, his elevated station in life was the most prideful event in Mom's life. She told everyone about her familial relationship to this man who was in all the newspapers and on television all of the time. Mom could only interpret my failure to be a Griffin cheerleader, and my refusal to bask in the reflected glory of a family relationship, as evidence that I was jealous of Jimmy Griffin and of his success. A tension over this issue grew between Mom and me, that persisted even to the moment of her death.

After Mom's funeral and estate settlement, I returned to the United Way, but there was only a few days of the UW campaign remaining. Then I returned to City Hall, but this time I reported to Joe Schollard, Commissioner of Inspections and Licenses, for assignment. Schollard's departmental responsibilities had recently been expanded to include the redevelopment of city-owned vacant land. Schollard welcomed my presence on his staff. He acknowledged that my experience in scattered site housing development, my knowledge of federal and state housing regulations, and my familiarity with local, state and federal housing officials, could provide him with invaluable assistance in completing his new responsibilities. In addition, Joe Schollard was a decent man. Never again would I be subjected to systematic harassment. Both Schollard and I acknowledged that it was in our mutual self-interest that I maintain the lowest possible profile in any departmental activity.

Over the next few years, Commissioner Schollard formulated and conducted a scattered site housing program, Pratt-Whitney Neighborhood Restoration Program, that was eventually deemed to be a model for inner-city new housing construction programs across the nation. With the exception of three months in 1989, when I was once again assigned to the United Way as a loaned executive, I principally operated as Joe Schollard's (secret) aide-de-camp. One day Schollard said to me, "The Mayor asked me what work I had assigned you."

I asked, "What did you tell him?"

"I just said that I was assigning you every dirty job that I could find and those that no one else on the staff knew how to do," he replied.

"What was the Mayor's response?" I questioned.

"Pleased as punch," responded a broadly grinning Commissioner Schollard.

During the Summer '87, the City was employing a large number of welfare dependent workers, who were paid minimal wages and assigned menial or simple clerical tasks. On my infrequent visits to Schollard's office I noticed an attractive young woman who was invariably pleasant and who was obviously being assigned more responsible tasks each week. Our personal relationship was confined to exchanging greetings and an occasional pleasantry about the weather, lack of air conditioning or impending rain. We never had the occasion to discuss "business" matters, and never conversed about anything of a personal nature.

Late in the summer, one of the women in Schollard's office mentioned that 'Carolyn' was returning to school in a few days. The news that Carolyn was not a 'welfare' worker, but was a student intern surprised me. I left a note on Carolyn's desk stating that she had been a pleasure to work with and wishing her success in her future studies. Later in the day, Carolyn came to my office, for the first time, thanked me for my note and asked if it would be all right if she telephoned me occasionally. I said "Sure,—anytime!".

What followed Carolyn's departure from City Hall was a series of casual phone conversations, interrupted by an occasional coffee klatch, where Carolyn would relate her scholastic achievements and puzzlements, as well as collegiate experimentation in social intercourse. A few times Carolyn made social missteps which placed her in physical and moral peril. On these occasions, I would assume the role of parental scold, confessor, and/or mensch. To the best of my knowledge, Carolyn survived her entrance into adulthood without serious mishap or psycho-social scarring.

Once Carolyn began working full time, and became self sufficient, my role as pendant ceased, and we gradually became romantically involved. We continued to be circumspect and most of our trysts occurred in motels or out-of-town. Eventually, Carolyn met more suitable, and socially acceptable, romantic partners, and she and I resumed our former clandestine "companionship" status.

At that time, everything on my horizon looked promising and tranquil. I was winding up the Crescent Mortgage Corporation debacle. Barb and I had assisted in the purchasing of two additional residences. One was occupied by our daughter, Kate, and the other was the home of our son John and his family. Both properties were two-family homes so that each property was self-amortizing and no additional financial expenditure was required. I was playing some golf and some tennis. I began to visit casinos in Atlantic City, Las Vegas, Reno, and Syracuse, where I played blackjack almost exclusively. Sometimes I went with City Hall companions, a few times I was accompanied by Barb, and sometimes I took Carolyn, but mostly I gambled alone. I never made much money and I never lost any great sums. For me, gambling was an inexpensive (though dangerous) method of relaxation and solitude. I saw Carolyn occasionally. Barb and I frequently visited or went out with Buz and Irene Roberts. My days at City Hall were mundane, but free from harassment. I had lunch occasionally with Dick Miller, but I saw little of any others of the old Sedita crowd.

Then, almost imperceptibly, an unraveling began. My son John, and his family, purchased a single family home and moved out of the Parkside Avenue property. After a year or so of renting out both apartments, I decided to sell this large property and use the proceeds to purchase a Florida retirement residence for Barb and myself. I quickly received two offers for the property. One was from a young doctor and his wife who were going to use the first floor flat as medical office space, and the second floor apartment as their living quarters. The second offer received was from a single young man, who owned a West Side restaurant. The second offer was almost $10,000 higher than the doctor's offer, but the young man was saddled by business debts and expenses and he asked if I would hold a second mortgage and allow him to assume the FHA first mortgage that I had on the premises. I took the higher, and riskier offer! I calculated that the monthly income that I received in second mortgage payments would be sufficient for me to finance the purchase of a small Florida condominium.

After about a year, the tenants on the first floor of the Parkside Avenue residence moved and almost immediately second mortgage payments to me became infrequent and partial. Next, I was informed that the new owner was in serious arrears on his payments on the FHA mortgage. Soon, I received notice of foreclosure action from the first mortgagor. If the first mortgagor foreclosed, I would lose my entire income and principal from the second mortgage. I instituted legal action to foreclose on the second mortgage. In order to repossess the property I had to reassume the FHA mortgage amount, and I had to repay the bank all unpaid mortgage payments, plus penalties, plus interest. The original lender wouldn't allow me to refinance the first mortgage so that I had to add more than $12,000 to my credit card debt in order to regain title to the two family home.

I then compounded my difficulty by allowing the prior owner (who had defaulted) to occupy the second floor apartment (at a fair rent) until I could make the necessary repairs and refurbishing of the vacant, first floor apartment, in anticipation of my selling the property again! Once I had completed the modernization of the first floor apartment, and had spruced up the surrounding landscape, I placed the property in the hands of a realtor (for sale), but I received no offers whatsoever for this investment property.

After a few months, I discovered that the previous owner (now occupying the second floor apartment) had driven away all prospective buyers with his eccentric and crass behavior. I immediately had an eviction order issued but by the time that I was able to force this tenant to move, he had completely trashed the second floor apartment.

Fortunately, shortly thereafter I found a tenant for the first floor apartment, and my son Tom, committed himself to restoring the second floor apartment into livable condition. Tom not only worked feverishly and effectively to restore this apartment, he moved into the quarters, and has paid rent and provided stability, security and maintenance to the property to this day. I am forever grateful to Tom for relieving me of a responsibility that threatened to crush me financially and emotionally.

I still had to deal with the credit card debt that I had incurred when I first averted the foreclosure of the FHA mortgage. Fortunately, at this same approximate time, my daughter, Kate, and her husband, Dave, decided that they wished to sell her home in Kenmore and move to a larger residence in a more rural setting. The property was quicky sold and Barb, who was a co-owner, received a nice profit from the sale. I implored Barb to allow me to use her profit from the sale of Kate's home to reduce my credit card debt, which had been created when the Parkside property foreclosure was averted. Without any hesitation or recrimination, Barb gave me the money that I needed to 'get even'. I had also received a small amount of money from my parent's estates, which I used to eliminate another credit card balance, (residue of Crescent Mortgage Corp.).

A few days before my 60th birthday, I received the news that the civil service position of 'Project Coordinator' was being eliminated from the City of Buffalo budget. It was possible for Griffin to do this because by this time most of the Community Development staff, with identical or similar job titles to mine, had transferred to BURA, and were no longer carried on the City's payroll roster. There was no civil service position that I could move to, nor were there even further demotions available. I had been "hoisted with my own petard."

Like most people, I hadn't done anything while I was in City Hall that was remarkable. But, for a number of years, civic leaders let me believe that I had some important ideas and I was given free rein to do what I thought best for the citizens of Buffalo. Later, when I was subjugated into the political netherworld, I still believed that my ideas were worthy of serious consideration and I resented the fact that it was demonstrated to me on a daily basis that my opinions no longer mattered to anyone.

Now, I was being told that my time, and my presence, had no value to the City that I had served for a quarter of a century.

I decided that I had stayed at City Hall too long. I was tired of fighting and conniving. On my 60th birthday I retired,—and I never went back!

For the next two years, I continued a leisurely existence. I puttered around the Parkside property and around the homestead on Crescent Avenue. I saw Carolyn more frequently but our relationship became less romantic and more social with each passing day. Yet, since all of my children, and all of their friends, were now adult and about town at any time, our trysts became more secretive and far-flung in order to avoid scandal or embarrassment to anyone. It was becoming apparent to both of us that the amour had run its course. Carolyn had blossomed into a beautiful woman. She was anxious to marry and start her family. On the other hand, I was at the other end of the spectrum. It seems strange to say now what was true then…my marriage to Barbara was rock solid. There had never been any other 'love' in my life.

There may be some who think that I have behaved like something of a 'rake' during my marriage, but I don't believe the facts support this conclusion. While it is true that I continuously and fervently maintained close, personal relationships with several lovely women through the years, none of these friendships ever became 'affaires'. I have never patronized a brothel, nor have I ever participated in a 'one-night stand'. I've never picked up anyone in a bar, or anywhere else, nor have I engaged in 'casual sex'. I've been honored to have five ladies, each of them family friends or warm acquaintances, tell me that they had never broken their marriage vows and then say,"…but if I ever cheat with anyone it would be with you". Not once did I ever interpret this statement as an invitation, a proposal, or as a solicitation. In each instance, I believed that the innocent statement was meant to convey the respect and esteem that others felt for me. I never repeated to anyone what any of the ladies said to me, nor did I ever refer to the occasion again. But, in each instance, I was touched and honored by the remark. I held each of these ladies in the highest esteem before, during, and after the remarks.

Yet looking back, I now question whether I wanted to continue 'married' life. After all, Barb and I had married when we were both 20 years old, following a two-year courtship. I suspect that I yearned to return to youthful pursuits. I know that I fantasized that I could once again hook up with my St. Bonaventure play-mate, Red Hodson and that we could collaborate on writing a play, or producing a book. At the very least, Red and I could visit Las Vegas or Atlantic City and raise a little hell in our senior years. I was sure that Barbara would tolerate such outrageous behavior, even though I also knew that she shouldn't! But I wasn't sure that I wanted her to tolerate me any longer, either!

A few days before my 64th birthday, when Barb confronted me with evidence of my past indiscretion with Carolyn, there was no denial. I not only accepted blame but I admitted to other romantic (but not adulterous) liaisons and dalliances. One of my life's compartments had been breached and there was no way to avoid, ignore, or deny new disclosures. Every member of the family was soon involved. Many of my 'beloved' were outraged by my betrayal of their mother and were confused at my refusal to assign blame to Carolyn, or to show any contrition for my wanton behavior.

I thought at that time that I had fought to save our marriage. Today I'm not sure. I think that I might have let my most precious possession,—the love and respect of my family, slip away in order that I might recapture, or experience for the first time, the dubious pleasures of youth.

I believe that Barbara desperately wanted to save our marriage. But the loss of her best friend, the shattering of a lifetime's trust, and the memory of betrayal and falsehoods, leaves scars that cannot be erased.

I believe that Barb and I are still in love, but that our marriage has ended. And so I left Buffalo for life in Florida, alone.

EPILOGUE

In her poem, *"Success"*, Bessie Anderson Stanley included the lines, "He has achieved success who has lived well, laughed often and loved much; who has enjoyed the trust of pure women and the love of little children; who has filled his niche and accomplished his task; who has left the world a little better than he found it...; who has always looked for the best in others and given them the best that he had." I don't believe that I qualified as a success under Ms Stanley's criteria, but I really tried!

As I've attempted to edit my wistful memoir, *Growing Up and Growing Old in Buffalo NY,* I find more and more to add each day. But, rather than impede the narrative flow that made the original memoir such a joyful experience for me to read, I've collected my more visceral thoughts in a collection of essays which are included here as a concluding tome. Even though some of these recollections contain chaff I hope that they will add some insight, provide some humorous remembrances, or even provoke some serious thought in the reader.

RESTAURANTS AND TAVERNS

Today, it's dismaying to have to tell someone that Buffalo is my original "home town". A pall seems to envelope the room as my converser instinctively attempts to console me with phrases like, "I'm so sorry!" and "Does it really snow there all of the time?" and "I'll bet that you're glad to be out of there!".

Invariably I answer with, "You know it's funny, but Buffalo is a lousy place to visit for a week, because there's little for a visitor to do! On the other hand, Buffalo is a really great place in which to live! It has terrific residents, and nice residential neighborhoods, and sensational food in restaurants that visitors seldom visit!"

That's absolutely true! As I look back toward my youth, memories of meals enjoyed in Buffalo's ethnic neighborhoods and restaurants remain indelibly etched in my mind.

My earliest childhood memories are of spaghetti dinners at Chef's Restaurant on Seneca Street, at Onetta's Restaurant at Main and Bailey Avenue, and at The Anchor Bar on Main and North Streets. Buffalo is renowned for it's corner bars and saloons. It really seems as if there's one on every block. At the very least, one doesn't have to travel far to find a bar "where everyone knows your name" in Buffalo. And it seems that every corner tavern features "Fish Fry" every Friday night. I always assumed that the predominance of Italian, Polish and Irish Catholics made this a logical culinary selection, but it may have been the proximity to Lake Erie, and it's variety of delicious fresh water fish, that prompted the "Fishfry on Friday" tradition in Buffalo.

During World War II, there would be lines of 30 to 40 customers waiting for tables and standing outside the doors of "Roy's" and "Sargent's" restaurants on Friday nights, rain or shine, winter or summer. Both restaurants were located at the foot of Ferry Street, west of Niagara Street and both specialized in "Lake Erie" fish dishes, such as yellow perch, bass and pike. When our family went out for fishfry, we generally went to "Leonard's Restaurant" on Delavan Ave, near Humboldt Pkwy. Leonard's was usually less crowded, while serving an excellent 'battered' fishfry. And occasionally, we would cross the Peace Bridge, or take the ferry to Fort Erie Ont., to enjoy 'fish and chips'. I've often wondered why American restaurants didn't offer white vinegar to put on french fries (chips). It enhances the flavor so much!

During the late 1930's and 1940's, Buffalo was dotted with "Deco Restaurants", serving "Buffalo's Best Cup of Coffee" for a dime. There were also some "White Tower" 'diner type' locations which specialized in hamburgers, and a very few "Toddle House", a very tiny diner, serving better coffee than Deco, and better hamburgers than White Tower, in my opinion. After WWII, "Your Host Restaurants" began opening 'coffee shoppes' all over Western New York and this 'new' concept eventually became so dominant that the individual diner and Deco-type stand became 'almost extinct'.

During my high school years, my friends and I frequented "Riviera Restaurant", a small, almost always empty, Italian restaurant located on Franklin Street, directly behind the Sheas Buffalo Theater. We usually enjoyed a plate of 'spaghetti, with meat sauce', either before or following a visit to a downtown theater.

But in my late teens it was far more common for us to meet, or to congregate in neighborhood bars and taverns, than to dine in restaurants. "Whiteys" at Main and Delevan and "Parkside Lounge" were hangouts for the Canisius College crowd.. We split our lounging time between "JayBees" on Amherst Street near Grant St. (Jachimiak's neighborhood), "Hagerty House" on Hertel Ave., near Delaware Ave, "Checkers" on Hertel Ave near Norwalk (Killeen's neighborhood) and "Parkside Lounge" (Irwin's neighborhood). While "Santora's" on Main Street had good pizza, the very finest, thin and cheesy, was served at the "Bocce Club" restaurant on Eagle Street. Hot roast beef sandwiches, on kimmelweck rolls, were served in German restaurants all over town, but we favored those served at "Meyers" on Delaware, near Delevan.

And finally, delicious one foot long, charcoal broiled 'hot dogs', were to be had at "Pat's" on Sheridan Drive and Colvin Avenue. Each Buffalo Neighborhood had a candy shop, or drug store with a soda fountain, to serve sodas, sundaes, and milkshakes. In North Buffalo there were two "Parkside Candy Shoppe" locations where a variety of chocolates, candies, and ice cream treats could be enjoyed in quaint 'booths'. "Ryan's Drug Store" on Main Street at Coe Place (very near old St. Joe's) served what was generally conceded to be 'the best milkshakes in town'.

Great dining experiences, at affordable prices, have been the hallmark of the Buffalo area since World War II.. My family and I resided in North Buffalo during my entire adult life, so most of dining was done in restaurants in the northern portion of the city and in northern Erie County. We patronized many of the fine restaurants that were established on Delaware Ave. "Round Table", "The Chateau", "Victor Hugo's", Peter Gust's "Park Lane", "Olivers" and "Saratoga", all featured excellent cuisine, fine service, and a genteel atmosphere. "Rue Franklin", Buffalo's only french restaurant, served exquisite food in intimate surroundings. In the suburbs, we particularly enjoyed the warmth, hospitality and diverse menu at "Hour Glass" on Kenmore Ave, but we also spent many enjoyable evenings at "Syracuse Restaurant", "Little White House", "Coachman's", "Charter House", and "Salvatore's Italian Gardens", with family and friends. Barb and I regularly accompanied Buz and Irene Roberts in visits to Chef's Restaurant for delicious Italian food.

Fort Erie, Ont., just over the Peace Bridge, was the location of six or seven excellent Chinese restaurants. And it seemed that all Buffalo diners visited John's Flaming Heath Restaurant in Niagara Falls NY at least once each year for a succulent steak dinner, accompanied by icebox pumpkin pie for dessert. During the summer months, all of the area country clubs offer a varied, and excellent cuisine, however I've never had better food anywhere than the meals routinely served at the Westwood Country Club.

I know that there were fabulous fish-fry to be had on the Lake Shore Blvd, Hoak's Restaurant comes immediately to mind. Orchard Park and East Aurora were noted for their fine restaurants. But these weren't convenient to North Buffalonians, and we simply didn't frequent those establishments when other fine restaurants were more conveniently located near our home.

The principal difficulty with remembrances of this kind, is that I know that I've enjoyed fabulous meals at Buffalo restaurants whose name I've now forgotten, and that there are hundreds of great restaurants in the Buffalo area that I never frequented or even visited. All that I can attest to is that Western New York is a great place in which to live, to work, to play, and to dine.

LITERATURE

It seem to me that I have been reading' books' for my entire life. My first clear recollection is reading a series of adventure novels about *"Don Winslow of the Navy"* and *"Bulldog Drummond"* mysteries in the late 1930's, before World War II. I found the hardcover novel to be more engrossing than the 'dime' comic books that were being introduced in those days. Needless to say, I also had my stash of comic books and of 'war cards' which constituted a kind of currency among young boys on Buffalo's West Side. Each could be collected, traded or bartered. While there was no formal "market", we seemed to instinctively know and agree that a 'Superman' ACTION comic book was worth two or more "Captain America" or Plastic Man" comics. And I never knew any kid who collected "Wonder Woman" books.

With the entry of America into World War II my reading habits turned to the 'war news'. I vividly recall how Ernie Pyles dispatches from North Africa, then Europe, informed, entertained, comforted and reinforced the resolve of the nation throughout the war years. Pyle's column, which was printed each night in the Buffalo Evening News, between the radio listings and Bill Mauldin's wartime cartoons of 'Willie and Joe' or the Stars and Stripes cartoon figure "Sad Sack", was a 'must read' for me. I also recall that I borrowed two Ernie Pyle books from the Public Library, *"Brave Men"* and *"Here is Your War: Story of GI Joe"*. Later I purchased the book, *"The Story of Ernie Pyle"*.

During my high school days, and while attending St. Bonaventure University and the University of Buffalo, I could be best described as "an indifferent student". I effortlessly received middle grades (B's and C's) which allowed me to do, or to avoid, whatever I chose. I remained, however, an incessant reader. The paperback novel (35 cents) was introduced in the late 1940's, and I remember that I, and my friends, couldn't get enough of Mickey Spillane's *"I the Jury"* and *"My Gun is Quick"*.

Also, with the end of World War II, a host of journals and diaries were published. For some time I had been fascinated by the efficiency and ruthlessness of the German War Machine, and I remember the relish with which I began reading Joseph Goebbels' *"Diaries."*. Much to my surprise, I found that during those horrific war years, the Nazi Minister of Propaganda was as much concerned with the decrease in the number of German movies being imported by Romania, and the lack of foodstuffs and shelter for the residents of Hamburg, following British air raids, as he was about the morale of German troops on the Russian front, or other political and military problems. In fact, I recall that in these private diaries, Goebbels claimed that the German Air Force bombed British civilians in retaliation for British 'terror bombing' of Hamburg, Germany. But the everlasting impression left on me by this book was the imposing charisma of Adolf Hitler. Time and time again, Goebbels would become despondent, sometimes to the point of panic, over military failures, or political pressures, or even the efficacy of Nazi policy. He would be prepared to unburden his woes upon Hitler. But then the next day's diary entry would begin,—"Yesterday I saw the "Fuehrer"!!! It was wonderful!! He assured me that everything is going well and according to plan!!! We must all work harder to insure Germany's success!!" Never did Hitler fail to calm, to charm, or to enchant his most loyal vassal.

Other books that I remember reading in my teens included, *Stalin: Czar of the Russias"* and *"Genghis Khan"*. One book that had an immediate and lasting impact was entitled *"Murder Inc"*. by Burton Turkus. This book chronicled the grisly careers of "Lucky" Luciano, Frank Costello, Alphonse Anastasia, and Abe ("Kid Twist") Reles., presaging the cast and plot of the "Keefaufer Committee' televised hearing on organized crime, a few years later.

The early 1950's produced a spate of World War II journals and chronicles. After reading William Shirer's books *"End of a Berlin Diary"* and *"The Rise and Fall of the Third Reich"*, Winston Churchill's six volume *The Second World War"*, General Eisenhower's *"Crusade in Europe"*, and Barbara Tuchman's *"Stilwell and the American Experience in China 1911–45"*, I came to the conclusion that Roosevelt was as wily and crafty as a man could get, Churchill was a pompous pettifogger who wasn't capable of admitting to making any mistakes in the conduct of WWII, Eisenhower might be the "luckiest" man ever born, Hitler's charisma (and madness) was confirmed, Stalin was a brutal "thug" and Chiang Kai-shek was an incompetent, corrupt "gangster".

By the late 1950's I was working full time, but still attending the University of Buffalo at night. My reading taste turned to books about 'business' or 'salesmanship'. However I recall that one of my UB classes introduced me to the economist

Thorstein Veblen's book, *"The Theory of the Leisure Class"*. I only remember that this book introduced the concept of "conspicuous consumption" to me and induced in me a lifelong fascination with the 'dead science' of economics. Robert Heilbroner, another economist, wrote, "Veblen's theory of the leisure class is to be compared to that of Marx's theory. Marx was of the view that the upper class were at "swords points" with one another and the inevitable historical outcome would be the violent overthrow of the upper classes. Veblen, however, was of the view that the lower classes were not out to over throw the upper class; but rather, strived up to it." In any event, I was 'hooked'!

I soon absorbed John Kenneth Galbraith's book, *"The Great Crash"* and over the next decade I purchased and read Galbraith's *"Affluent Society"*, *"Economics and the Public Purpose"*, *"The Age of Uncertainty"* and *"The New Industrial State"*. I was impacted tremendously by each of Galbraith's books. To say that I was infected by "a liberal bias" is a vast understatement! I didn't confine my economic reading to Galbraith. Over the years I purchased and read several economic texts by Robert Heilbroner, including: *"The Great Ascent; the Struggle for Economic Development in Our Time"*; *"Between Capitalism and Socialism: Essays in Political Economics"*; *"Beyond Boom and Crash"*; *"Behind the Veil of Economics: Essays in the Worldly Philosophy"*; and *"The Crisis of Vision in Modern Economic Thought"*. My current favorite economic writers are Robert Reich, (*The Future of Success*) and Paul Krugman (*The Great Unraveling*).

I realize that this listing is both exhausting and extremely pedantic Many times. I've been told by people working, or studying other professions,—law, engineering or medicine-, that the study of economics is "boring". And I must admit that in all of the economic texts that I've read, I never learned how to make even 'one thin dime'. But what I did learn was that almost every human endeavor, whether it be in the 'arts', or politics, government or 'making war', or even education and athletics, has at it's roots an economic rational. I can't think of a single thing that has been accomplished that didn't have an economic purpose and effect.

While earning my livelihood, I also found time to read Bruce Catton's *"Army of the Potomac Trilogy: Mr Lincoln's Army/Glory Road/Stillness at Appomattox"*, as well as other historical novels and biographies, but soon the stories of current political struggles made the Civil War seem ancient and dull. *"The Making of the President—1960"* by Theodore White changed the way that political campaigns were covered, as much as the 1960 campaign changed the political process and landscape, and infused thousands of young people, including me, to become interested in politics and active in government affairs. The subsequent "Making of the President" books reinforced the concepts that 'government service' could be both honorable and personally rewarding.

It also seems that during the 1960's the nation's awareness of the rights and abilities of individual citizens came into a much sharper focus. And it wasn't only the 'hippies' and the 'flower children' who experienced this growing social awareness. Studs Terkel wrote a series of oral histories, *"Hard Times"* (interviews with people about Great Depression experiences), *"Working"* (people's working lives) and *"The Good War"* (World War II) which were best sellers and which were extremely sensitive to the needs, the desires, and the accomplishments of America's working class. Michael Harrington's *"The Other America: Poverty in America"* pricked the conscience of President Kennedy and of the populace, and paved the way for massive government spending to assist the elderly, the unemployed and unemployable, and other unfortunate families in attaining a dignified and decent standard of living.

The murder of John F Kennedy, and the subsequent horrific *"Warren Commission Report"* gave rise to a new cottage industry, the writing and publishing of theories of 'how' JFK was killed, 'who' was responsible, and the methods of cover-up used to conceal the identities of the assassins. The list of these "Conspiracy Theory" books is exhaustless, and will not be attempted here.

It is suffice to say that I bought and read most these books and that I believed most of what I read.. To this day, I'm not sure who killed President Kennedy, but I never will believe that an unmotivated loner (Oswald) planned and carried out the killing, calmly escaped the scene and then murdered a policeman when confronted hours later, miles away from the crime scene. The fact that Oswald denied any involvement in the assassination and requested 'an attorney' in his only appearance before reporters, that "Oswald's interrogation was not taped and no stenographer was present" (Associated Press Nov 21,1997), made the whole story 'suspect' to say the least. Parading the alleged 'assassin' in front of television cameras to be shot by a Chicago 'gunsel' while the assassin is in the firm grasp of Dallas detectives, and then the gunmen stating that his only motivation for shooting Oswald was that he (Ruby) wanted "To spare the beautiful widow (Jackie Kennedy) from the stress that a trial would cause her" would be 'high comedy' if it was presented in any other context.

In later years the murders of Martin Luthur King Jr and Robert Kennedy, again by two apolitical, ethnically neutral, unmotivated, lone (without organizational support) gunmen and the absence of any 'public' trials, led me to conclude that we had witnessed a coup d'etat. Nothing that has happened since, nor anything that I've read or seen, has caused me to change my mind about who really benefitted from the events of 11/22/63 in Dallas, TX

1963 also seemed to me to be the last year when this nation enjoyed the luxury of 'truth in government'. Before then when a US government official spoke, particularly the President, I believed what was said. I maybe didn't agree with what was said, maybe I didn't want to hear what was said, and maybe sometimes I suspected that the whole story wasn't being told, but I believed that what I was being told was true.. But then, in the 1964 campaign LBJ badly distorted the positions that his political opponent, Barry Goldwater, espoused. LBJ then followed with an unbelievable Tonkin Bay story as a rational for bombing North Vietnam cities and populations. He exaggerated 'body counts', and excelled in "Domino Theory" incantations. President Johnson was followed by Richard (Tricky Dick) Nixon, who first promised that he had a 'secret' plan for ending the war in Viet Nam, then bombed Cambodia and followed with the machinations which eventually led to his resignation in disgrace. *"The Pentagon Papers"*, released to the press by Daniel Ellsberg, and Woodward and Bernstein's *"All the President's Men"* revealed that Nixon and his underlings were more devious and corrupt than even I had previously thought.

David Halberstan, in his book *"The Best and the Brightest"*, described better times and better men serving in public office. *"The Fire in the Lake: the Vietnamese and the Americans in Vietnam"* by Frances Fitzgerald, provided both a historical perspective and the most comprehensive and compelling description of the vagaries, contradictions and conflicts confronting US troops and government while fighting this nasty war.

But these were fertile times for writers. Kurt Vonnegut was turning out small books each year. I began by reading *"Slaughterhouse—Five"* and again, I was hooked. I quickly bought and read, *"Player Piano"*, *"The Sirens of Titan"*, *"Cat's Cradle"*, *"God Bless You, Mr Rosewater"*, *"Breakfast of Champions"*, *"Slapstick"* and *"Deadeye Dick"*. Vonnegut became my moral compass during the troubled 1960's and 1970's. His antiwar, anti-establishment, amoral humor led me to the existentialist writing of Camus and Sartre. I read several books by each of these men but

I got very little out of my reading. I think that I'm an existentialist, but I don't know what an existentialist is!

There were other books, which told much less complicated tales. Four books by Robert Caro, *"Robert Moses: The Power Broker";* and *"The Years of Lyndon Johnson: The Path to Power; "Means of Ascent"; "Master of the Senate"* chronicled the political careers of two of the 20ᵗʰ Century's most powerful men, and described, in delicious detail, the Machiavelian processes they used to attain their prominence.

Finally, I would be remiss if I failed to mention the book that had the most profound and lasting influence on me throughout the years, *"Drama Critics Circle Award Plays".* I don't remember the year that it was published and I'm quite sure that it's out of print now. This book included the script and casts for each of the award winning plays, as well as a summary of the critics voting, and a list of each contending play, for each year. I'm not sure but I think that "Winterset" was the first play included in the book, and I'm sure that the latest Drama Critics Circle Award winner in this edition was "A Cat on a Hot Tin Roof". Only a synopsis of 'Cat' was included so that this gives some indication of the time frame that was covered. I only know that I read, and reread each play, until all the pages were dog-eared and worn almost to transparency. Some plays, like "Picnic", Death of a Salesman", "Streetcar Named Desire" or "All My Sons" were almost committed to memory. In any event this single book invested in me a love of 'theater' that persists to this day.

And my addiction to 'reading' is unabated!

PARENTING

George Bernard Shaw once wrote, "Parentage is a very important profession, but no test of fitness for it is ever imposed in the interest of the children".

Most of us become parents at a relatively young age. We enter this blissful state with high expectations for the future well being of our children. But there is no school which teaches the art of parenting. Often the experience of prior generations is of little value in a world where mores, habits and customs seem to be as changeable as television channels. And our elders really didn't have much to teach us because they were so busy getting through each day of parenting, that they forgot to learn much about what they were doing. It's truly amazing that our children turn out as well as they do!

I never knew either of my grandfathers. My mother's father died when she was a very young child, and he was seldom mentioned in my home or recollected at family gatherings. My grandfather Murphy died when I was a toddler. He was universally and invariably referred to as "a mean old sonofabitch".

My father was undoubtedly a better father, and probably a better husband, than my grandfather ever was. I think that I was a better father to my children than my father was to me. And I certainly expect that my sons, and sons-in-law, will be better to, and for their children, than I was to mine.

These statements are neither accusatory nor apologetic, for it must be recognized that standards and conditions change with each generation and it is grossly unfair to measure twentieth century behavior against twenty-first century standards. Different nationalities and ethnics follow different customs and child rearing traditions and to believe that there is only one true method of upbringing is pure folly. To cite just a few generational differences: I played on basketball teams representing my elementary school, the parish CYO, and my high school from 1946 to 1950. During that time, no one's father attended a practice session, and I was aware of only three fathers who attended any of the games played in order to watch their son's performance,—Pete Irwin's father, Bill Poorten's father and my father! Admittedly, there might have been fathers in attendance that I didn't recognize, but we don't have the time or the space here to list the fathers that I would have recognized if they had appeared at even one game! Does this mean that the absent fathers didn't love their sons as much as William Poorten Sr did? Or that Bus Irwin and Tom Murphy Sr loved their sons more than any of my other teammates were loved? Of course not!

As a young father, I coached a bit of Little League baseball, and some basketball. I attended a few hockey games to watch my sons, but I didn't play golf with any of them until they had reached their adulthood. Did this mean that I loved my sons more than other fathers, who were not in as good physical condition as I was, or had less leisure time available to them, or who just didn't enjoy baseball or hockey? Did I love my sons less than another father who took his son out to a golf course every summer day? Did my failure to provide dancing, piano or tennis lessons for my daughters indicate that I favored my sons or had greater affection for sons than for my daughters? Each of these questions is patently ludicrous, yet today's father is expected to attend every game, practice session and performance of every child, at any time, in any place, and at any cost. This is an admirable practice and I think that both parent and offspring benefit from the closer social contact. But we shouldn't measure a parent's devotion solely on the basis of attendance at his offsprings recreational activities.

I didn't know of any of my friend's fathers who did the cooking, washed the dishes, or performed any routine housekeeping tasks. My father didn't, and I never helped Barb with any of the daily household chores. My father-in-law, an extremely decent man, never even took the ashes or garbage cans to the curb, citing a suspected hernia suffered as a young man! But I also didn't know of anyone's mother who was employed outside the home! With the generations born before World War II, there was a separation of responsibilities, Dad was the wage earner and occasional handyman and Mom was the full-time homemaker, chief cook and bottlewasher. Today's two-earner households demand, and have every right to expect, a different breakdown of responsibilities, but it is grossly unfair to measure past generations performances against today's needs and standards.

I never viewed any authority,—legal, religious or parental-, nor any authority figure, as 'inspired' or 'inspiring'. I respected my Dad, I listened when he offered advice or gave me instructions. But, he was not my friend, he was my father,—the rule maker, teacher, final arbitrator of what was right or wrong, and occasional disciplinarian. I could not imagine discussing my personal problems with him,—that's what friends and priests are for! I would not think of arguing with, or criticizing my father, his opinions or his actions. I seldom sought his approval, nor did I always follow his advice or honor his dictates. Yet, my attitude should not be construed as reflecting any lack of affection or esteem for my father.

I don't recall ever asking anyone's permission to take any action, except that I would never use my father's car, or anyone else's property, without permission. And regardless of whether I had asked for prior approval, I always knew that I, and only I, was responsible for errors, mistakes or any other misfortune that befell me. I believe that I always accepted full responsibility for any of my activities, actions or statements, regardless of the consequences. It always seemed to me that any 'lie' was evidence of 'fear', and I don't believe that I was ever consciously afraid of anyone.

By the same token, I tried not to impose undue restrictions on the actions of any of my children. I had complete confidence that the decency, good judgement and common sense that each of them displayed on a daily basis would continue throughout their lifetimes. It never occurred to me that any of the children might misinterpret "permissiveness' as 'lack of caring' and I never had any reason to believe that any child of ours suffered from 'lack of attention'. I was confident that any of the children would seek assistance from me, or their siblings, if assistance was needed. I relied on their intelligence to assure them that any help that was requested, would be forthcoming without criticism, or complaint. Never, not for even an instant, could I conceive that any of my children would ever lie to me.

I never attempted to become 'a friend' to any of my children. I was their father, and that was a unique and awesome responsibility. I didn't expect to discuss with them their romantic dalliances, personal grudges, cosmetic imperfections, or persecutions by supervisors or teachers. I wanted them to know, and I think that I demonstrated on a couple of occasions, that I supported them in everything that they attempted. I tried to avoid ever being judgmental. I hoped that they knew that I was always on their side in any and every dispute outside the family circle, whether they be right or wrong, and regardless of whether we had any hope of winning. I never wanted any of my children to take any action, or to express any opinion, solely "in order to please me". I tried to demonstrate that while I could be disappointed for my children, I was never disappointed in any of my children. I am proud of the fine adults that each of my children has become. I will always trumpet the fact that it was due to their efforts, and to their character, and to their love for each other, that they became "successful human beings". I tried, all of my life, to avoid doing anything that would disgrace, disappoint or disparage any member of my family, and I believe that each family member held themselves to this same high standard.

I believed that I had a responsibility to be a 'moral compass', to set a good example and to provide the guidance that all young people require. But I also was cognizant that a parent can only point the way (bend the twig), nourish and encourage, and eventually applaud the achievements of the child. Their parents are no more deserving of praise for the virtues and achievements of Mother Teresa or Albert Schweitzer, than the parents of Adolf Hitler or Ted Bundy can be condemned for the sins of their children.

But I've come to believe that the only true happiness in life comes from 'knowing' that you are loved.. And it is in this respect that I sometimes fear that I may have failed my children. I was never demonstrably loving, or even affectionate. I relied on my children's common sense, and some interior spiritual voice, to tell them that I loved each of them dearly. And I maintained this attitude even after some dear friends of mine confided in me that they never knew if their parents loved them. I would caution my children that if they love their offspring that they not presume that common sense will prevail,—make sure that each child knows that he or she is loved by you.

I also always presumed that each of my children realized that while my instructions and advice to them was well meant and loving, that I was not "infallible"—I could be wrong! To this day, my daughter Linda bristles when I refer to her as "my favorite", but since she was a little girl, she was the only one of my offspring who would challenge my assumptions, debate my declarations, and force me, through the power of her argument, to alter my directives. Linda wasn't always right either, but without her forthrightness and sometimes righteous indignation, I would have made a lot more paternal mistakes than I did!

Parenting is best performed in the company of an intelligent, loving and sympathetic partner! This is not said in a jocular fashion. I was blessed by having Barb at my side whenever any important decision had to be made. Each issue was fully discussed before any corrective action was taken. Our first, and foremost consideration, when any problem arose, was for the security and sake of the individual child. Secondly, but of prime importance, we always tried to enlist the informed support of each family member for any disciplinary action that was taken. I never remember Barb and I being in basic disagreement over a course of action or later appearing to be a reluctant or unwilling participant in a disagreeable resolution of a problem. We certainly never practiced any "good cop vs bad cop" routine. Nor did either of us ever utter the words, "Wait until I tell your father (or mother) what you've done!" or "I wish your father (or mother) hadn't done that!".

Occasionally I have dreamed. Seldom, if ever, have I experienced nightmares, and only a few of my dreams are memorable, There is one exception,—during my thirties and forties I had a recurring dream,—maybe six times,—maybe a dozen times. It's particulars are always the same, with variants only at the end of the dream. The provenance of the dream is obviously the movie "The Next Voice You Hear", starring James Whitmore and I believe, Nancy Davis (later America's First Lady, Mrs. Ronald Reagan). This movie, made in the late 1940's, was not a big hit, nor remarkable in any way. I doubt that anyone else but me has remembered it at all!

The Dream:

> On Sunday evening, TV broadcasting worldwide is interrupted by the announcement that "GOD" is going to make an announcement. Almost immediately the image of Jesus Christ, wearing a crown of thorns, appears in the sky. Jesus speaks wearily, "I've given you sun, water, food,—all of the things needed to make life on Earth pleasant.—And all that I've asked in return is that you love your fellow man and obey my Commandments but you always want more and are never satisfied. Even though I've sent floods, and war, and disease to warn you of my displeasure, you persist in your sinning. I've had enough!! On Saturday evening I'm ending the world and all life on Earth will cease!"

> With that Jesus takes the crown of thorns from his brow, hurls it to the ground, turns on his heel and fades from sight.

> (Still in the dream) My next recollection is awakening the next morning. What does one do? Go to church? To pray and ask forgiveness for sins and promise to never sin again?Give alms to the poor, or go hug a Negro, an Arab, or a Jew? (This seems a little hypocritical…besides, I think GOD will see right through the sham) Perhaps I should revise my will, or sell my house and my stocks and bonds, or purchase more life insurance. It seems so silly when one remembers that on the following weekend (and forever more) there will be no stock exchange, or banks, nor will there be anyone to measure the number of toys or the amount of assets I possessed when the world ended. Nor will there be any family members to enjoy the fruits of my labors and sagaciousness. Should I go to my job? Visit customers or co-workers? Start a diet? Play golf? Learn to swim or dance? Say goodbye to family, friends or loved ones?

No,—in each dream, after dismissing all of these futile activities, I opted to seek out and spend the final days with a loved one,—doing and saying the things that I hoped to, or should have done or said at some future date, or perhaps had neglected to do in the past,—trying to describe to them, lives and loves that they would never experience!!.

End of the Dream.

The obvious quandary posed in each of these dreams is who does one chose to share the last hours of the earth's existence and all of life's secrets with? I honestly do not remember who I spent those final fantasia hours with! I seem to recall sessions with my sons, maybe some grandsons, and maybe some of my daughters. I have no recollection of what we did, or what was said. What made the dreams so memorable was the transitory nature of those needs, desires and ambitions that we treasure and which dominate our everyday lives. Of course, what the dream reveals is my personal need to convey what I've learned about life to future generations, and how I have invariably delayed in fulfilling that need. It probably also denoted my fear that my death would occur before I had accomplished my parental responsibilities. I'm old now and yet there are still countless things that I'd like to be able to say to my children, and to my grandchildren. And there are at least as many things that I'd like to learn from those much younger, and wiser than I. In his 87th year, the artist Michelangelo is believed to have said, "Ancora Imparo"("I am still learning"). I would like to think that I share in this sentiment.

I liked all of my grandchildren, which was easy since I didn't have the responsibility of "parenting" them. I deeply regret that I never had the opportunity of "knowing" any of my grandchildren for I believe that I've mellowed as I've aged, and I think that I now have the time and the inclination to share thoughts, ideas, and doubts with them. It is among my fondest hopes that one or more of my grandchildren will read this memoir, will get to know a little about me, and will profit in some way from this knowledge.

ENTITLEMENTS

The generation that preceded mine, my parents, teachers, clergy, mentors, supervisors, advisors and government officials, were born before the year 1925 and knew America as "The land of opportunity". They recognized that long hours of hard work, and a little bit of luck were required for a person to survive, let alone prosper, in this nation. They also saw that a few men, with callous disregard for the law, or with brutality, and without moral principals, sometimes could attain powerful positions of authority, or fabulous wealth, or both.

The men and women of this 'lost' generation, had little expectation of attaining riches, and they quickly learned the indignities imposed by poverty when they experienced the October 1929 stock market crash and saw good jobs and wages disappear overnight and were reduced to standing in bread lines, soup kitchens and welfare queues. Many of them knew the chill and bitterness that occurs when one cannot buy a new Christmas toy, or warm clothes, or sometimes a decent meal for their loving wife and children. These experiences were forever seared in the collective memories of those who lived then. 'Frugality' was considered one of life's necessities, and 'fear of poverty' became a fact of life. There was a growing appreciation that the average working man, and his family, needed protection by the government from the avariciousness of giant corporations. They applauded FDR's New Deal that provided Social Security benefits to all, a social and financial safety net for those without work, and the promise of national health insurance in the future. The Wagner Act of 1935, which gave employees the right to organize (into unions), choose their own representatives, and to bargain collectively, was hailed as the emancipation of the American worker.

Then in the early 1940's, men, who were only a few years older than I, were called to fight in World War II. These men, now referred to as "The Greatest Generation", were the first to receive benefits under the GI Bill. A grateful nation provided veterans with low down payment and low interest mortgages, relief from property taxes, minimum cost life insurance, decent, affordable, lifetime medical attention, and free tuition, books and living expenses for those desiring a college education. Not one of these men felt 'privileged' when they received these benefits, for they had sacrificed time, their limbs, and sometimes the lives of their friends, in the service of our country. Careers, marriages and offspring had been delayed,—opportunities lost, sometimes never to be regained. Few of those who were not eligible for the veterans benefits resented the benefits that were bestowed, nor did anyone measure or object to the cost of the programs. These deserving young men, and their families, were the first generation of Americans who assumed that they were 'entitled' to a good life. Home ownership, or a new car, or a college education, was now viewed as compensation for hard work, not merely the reward for good luck, or fortunate breeding.

After World War II, "The Man in the Gray Flannel Suit" replaced "The Great Gatsby" as the nation's model of success. Union officials worked tirelessly, and sometimes spilled their blood, to improve the working conditions in the nation's mines, factories, and mills. Eventually, the sweatshops, six day work week, and ten hour work day became a faded memory of the 'Lost Generation'.

In the interest of full disclosure I must report that neither I, nor any of my ancestors, nor any of my descendants, benefitted in any way from any of the aforementioned government programs, and I might therefore be deemed to be biased in my assessment of their value. I, and several of my children, attended SUNYAB, but other than that no one of my family was the beneficiary of public education. We paid tuition at parochial and Catholic high schools and colleges for each of our children. Neither I, nor my ancestors, nor my children served in the Armed Forces. So of course, none of us was eligible for low cost insurance, low interest mortgages, the GI Bill, nor medical treatment at Veterans hospitals. Yet I never begrudged payment of either New York State or federal income tax, nor property taxes. I neither needed, nor deserved the benefits provided veterans, the poor, or the unemployed. I also recognized that these programs made our communities better places for all to live, to work and to play and that it was simple justice that we all shared in the expense of providing these benefits to those that had earned them, as well as to those who needed them.

Today, in the twenty-first century, "Baby Boomers", those Americans born after World War II, children of the 'Greatest Generation' and grandchildren of the 'Lost Generation', many of whom had either espoused the 'flower children' life style, the drug culture, or fought in Viet Nam, or all of the above, seem to have brought a new meaning to the definition of "entitlement". Corporate compensation packages that include generous doses of options to purchase shares in a publicly traded company that 'can't miss growing into one of the world's 'giants', have made retirement at age 50, with a millionaire's lifestyle, not only a realistic dream, but the benchmark of a worker's success. Ownership of a new home, completely furnished, and with an attached two car garage filled with a Lexus (for her) and a Hummer (for him) seems to be the newlyweds idea of a startup plan for marriage. The average annual salary of a major league baseball player is more than $3 million and a second baseman, who batted .237 the previous season, feels "dissed" by an offer of only $700,000 increase in salary for the coming season. Yet, there seems to be a growing resentment toward extending 'entitlements' to the lower classes, or to the disadvantaged. It is no longer fashionable to believe, let alone to advocate, that every person living in America is entitled to basic health care, a good (and affordable) education, a decent home in a secure neighborhood, as well as a living wage and a safe place in which to work.

Today, it is taken for granted that the cost of all public services are inflated and excessive. "Middle income" Americans appear to think that the only thing wrong in our country, is that unwed mothers are either running to abortion clinics every month or they're having babies every year, threatening eventually to bankrupt the Medicaid and Food Stamp programs. And it seems to be a national 'credo' that middle income tax rates are much too high and that high estate taxes have killed all incentives to invest in home-grown industries. Illegal immigration is tolerated, even encouraged, when it's explained that only foreign workers will work for wages that are insufficient to provide a decent standard of living in America.

There is a growing awareness that the cost of housing is exceeding the reach of the average working person, but there is steadfast opposition to raising the 'minimum wage rate'. There is an acknowledgment that many 'public housing' programs have failed, which seems to have fostered a growing sentiment that our government has no proper role to play in providing decent housing for low income workers. There seems to have been no concerted effort to find out why public housing has produced so many problems in America, while most European nations house as much as a third of their populations in public housing units. It may be un-American to spend federal tax dollars to provide decent housing for the poor, but woe to the elected US official who would dare propose that the income tax deduction for mortgage interest payments be eliminated in order to reduce the federal debt.

Almost fifty years ago, John Kenneth Galbraith contended in his book *"The Affluent Society"* that "A community can be as well rewarded by buying better schools and better parks as by buying more expensive automobiles". In other words, tax dollars spent on improved public facilities benefit the populace as a whole, yet resonate through the local economy in the same way that private investment, or expenditure of an individual's money, does. Galbraith went on to opine, "It is scarcely sensible that we should satisfy our wants in private goods with reckless abundance, while in the case of public goods…we practice extreme self-denial". Yet today, few seem willing to rescind recent cuts in income tax rates in order to rebuild, reinforce or rescue USA's railroads, bridges, levees, or urban infrastructures. Florida voters have rescinded their earlier approval of funds for the construction of a rapid rail system linking metropolitan centers across the state, in fear lest their tax rates be raised., while the sales of high priced condominiums and SUV's continue to soar. A federal program which would rebuild the nation's rail sytem, linking all major USA cities with rapid rail service would not only dramatically reduce the nation's reliance on imported oil, but would create hundreds of thousands of well paying jobs, that could only be performed in the States, and not exported to some Asian land.

We patriotically applaud when 'smart bombs' explode over Bagdad or other foreign cities, even though the cost of each of these 'bombs' exceed the cost of building a new school for our children.. There is little opposition to the $billions being spent to rebuild the oil rich Middle East nations, but our government seems to be growing more hesitant about spending the money necessary to create a safer, more livable New Orleans.. We seem to have forgotten that construction funds tend to remain in the tills of local merchants and pockets of local residents. Publically financed construction in Florida, or in Louisiana, can only be performed by American workers,—the jobs can't be outsourced overseas!

"Welfare Reform" is applauded when it requires single mothers to find employment outside the home in order to qualify for continued, but diminished, financial assistance from governmental agencies, while government funding for child care centers and "Head Start" programs are slashed in each federal budget year. The justification for the influx of foreign workers into the USA is that 'Americans' will not perform menial tasks for the low wages and under the poor working conditions that prevail in much of the nation today. Yet it is rare to hear protestation against "sweat shop" labor practices by local employers, or calls for improved working conditions and health benefits, for all of the workers in American. The news that some CEO's of large publicly owned corporations earn more salary in the hours before lunch on the first working day of the year, than the workers in the plant will earn during the entire 52 weeks of that year, is met by yawns, or questions of how one becomes a CEO!

It is most distressing to find that the hard earned benefits and learning of the "Lost Generation" are being gratuitously discarded by the "Babyboomers", who are running this nation and the world's giant corporations, today. These 'privileged few' are not entitled to remove the safety nets from beneath the underprivileged worker. They have not earned the right to deprive the less fortunate, the less talented, or the less industrious of the benefits that their fathers, and grandfathers, fought for and earned for all. When all of the governmental safety nets have been removed, what, and who will protect the American worker from free-falling into the abyss that the 'global economy' will bring to our shores?

EDUCATION

First, in retrospect, I must acknowledge, at least to myself, that I was never as good, or as accomplished, as I thought I was! I never achieved, anywhere near, what I was capable of! I've always been content 'to just get by'. I've never been driven 'to excel'.

I first attended school in 1938, Holy Angels Parochial School kindergarten conducted by the Grey Nuns. My final year of formal education was 1986, when I received a Masters Degree in Urban Planning at SUNYAB, School of Architecture. The years in between were spent in classrooms where, at various times, I received instruction from Sisters of St Joseph, Christian Brothers, Jesuits, Franciscans, as well as lay teachers at University of Buffalo (later SUNYAB), Bryant Stratton Business School, and Erie County Technical Institution (later Erie County Community College). I was a full-time student until 1954, when I began attending night school, and summer sessions at UB. At that time my curriculum became diverse, as I only took courses that interested me, or helped me in my work. My enrollments, though constant, were sporadic, for I also had to meet the needs and schedules of various employers and occupations. I don't remember taking any course because it offered easy credits, for I never had the attainment of a degree as the primary goal, or reward, of my college education. I'm not sure how or why I developed this attraction to education. It's often been stated that 'influences at home' are a primary determinate of the level of satisfaction, or accomplishment, that a youth derives from schoolwork. That doesn't appear to have been my prime motivation.

Neither of my parents were high school graduates. It is entirely possible that neither attended high school as we know it today. My father, Thomas J Murphy Sr, was born in Sault Ste Marie, Michigan and was raised on a farm until, as a young teenager, he accompanied his two older brothers when they ran away from home. The young men eventually found employment in Buffalo NY. I have heard Dad maintain that he attended South Park High School when he first arrived in Buffalo. But then, I also heard him claim that he had attended Michigan University.

My mother, born Catherine Griffin, attended St Mary's Business School after her graduation from St Brigid's Elementary School, in Buffalo's Old First Ward. Mom became an excellent typist and stenographer, and first gained full-time employment after one or two years of vocational training..

Mom was an avid reader of newspaper articles, particularly in her senior years, but neither she nor my father regularly read books or magazines. Though unlearned, both of my parents were intelligent, well-spoken, and versed in the social graces. However, having attained a modicum of success without formal education, they were not cognizant of the financial and social rewards that a college degree can bestow on a young person. I was not infused with any ambition to achieve academic greatness. I was always content to maintain a scholastic level that kept me from getting into trouble and which allowed me to study whatever I enjoyed most.

In most of my classrooms,. I scored very well on tests but I rarely did any homework, or participated in scholastic work outside of the classroom. I could best be described as an 'indifferent' student. But, I never remember the time that I wasn't engaged in reading one, or two books. And, as I recall, I enjoyed every hour of my educational experience.

In parochial school we attended classes that contained both boys and girls, and the teachers were invariably nuns. St. Joe's was a boy's high school, with the faculty predominately Christian Brothers, with only a smattering of lay teachers. When I attended St. Bonaventure Univ., I believe that there were only 13 females enrolled at the school, and the faculty once again was almost entirely composed of Franciscan priests. The University of Buffalo was of course co-ed, and there were no clerical faculty members. I've always believed that all-boys schools and all-girl schools gave each student body the best chance at scholastic success. I had seen enough preening and posturing in attempts to attract and impress the opposite sex to appreciate that removing these distractions from the classroom improved the 'esprit de corps' of the entire school, as well as the personal relationships between classmates. I neither experienced, nor ever heard of anyone experiencing erotogentic sensations from being deprived of the presence of the opposite sex during the school day.

In elementary school my highest marks were in arithmetic and mathematics, though if I were asked, I would have said that 'math' was one of my least favorite subjects. The one area of study where I had absolutely no interest or aptitude was 'any branch of science'. In every school, at every academic level, my lowest marks, and my complete lack of understanding and dexterity, was in any required science field. I soon came to the realization that I had all the scientific curiosity of "a rock"

My clear cut favorite subject in high school was plane geometry. I had been warned that this subject was nothing more than one semester of monotonous and taxing memorization. Students were initially required to memorize a series of axioms, and then were responsible for learning, by rote, an exhausting list of theorems, for it was certain that demonstrating the 'proof' of two theorems would be included in the final 'Regents' exam. When I arrived at my first class, I found that a new teacher had been hired.. We spent the first weeks in the classroom learning 'why' required axioms were "an established rule or principle, or a self evident truth". For example, once it was proven that parallel lines could 'never' cross each other, that axiom became a proven fact, and became one tool with which to construct solutions to larger problems, called theorums.. When the student had accumulated the total set of tools (axioms) it was possible to apply these axioms to solve, or prove, any theorum through deductive reasoning.

My studies in plane geometry became a microminiaturization of what I believe the process of 'education' should be. Schooling should consist of proving and learning indisputable facts (axioms), which can then be applied in later life to the resolution of a vast spectrum of diverse situations. When a student enters a Latin I or plane geometry classroom or chemistry lab for the first time, he is entering a world in which he has no previous knowledge, or experience. It is the responsibility of the 'teacher' to provide the tools, the indisputable facts, that will allow the student to translate, to puzzle, or to experiment, in order to find resolution to dilemmas, or intricate, but solvable 'unknowns'. For example, when studying History, remembering the dates that a war was fought, or which nation won the war, is not as important as discovering 'why' the war was fought, and whether the war could have been prevented.

The importance of education is that an "educated person" has learned 'to learn'. The educated person can face a problem in the work place, in the home, or in society in general, and through 'reason' (the application of indisputable facts) can attain a resolution that most benefits, or harms least, the situation. We have cheated our youth, by failing to help them to develop their ability "to learn".

Large portions of today's high-school graduates, and some college graduates, do not know how to read, or count, or reason. They are ill-equipped to contribute to society, or even to provide for themselves, much less to support a wife and family. Some of these youngsters are the first members of their families to have earned a high school diploma, and they are fiercely proud of what they've accomplished. But they are facing heartbreak and disappointment when they enter the workplace only to find that they are ill equipped to compete with foreigners for skilled positions and that others are willing to take on menial tasks for less than a living wage.

In college, I became fascinated by the wonders of economics. I took courses in Economics 101, Economic History of USA, Economic History of the World, Money and Banking, Public Finance, Microeconomics, Macroeconomics, Business Law, Investments, Real Estate and Insurance Law, and Personal Finance. I never learned how to become rich without working, but then, I never read any of Donald Trump's treatises either.

I returned to school at age 50, and earned a Masters Degree in Urban Planning at SUNYAB. I'm very proud of this accomplishment, although I must admit that while the work was difficult, and I worked hard to master the curriculum, I didn't learn much that was useful in Graduate School. I did discover that one of the reasons that students fail 'to learn' is the inability of some highly educated and intelligent people to communicate what they know to their students.

Macroeconomics was one of the 'elective' courses that I enrolled in during graduate studies. Economics had been my lifelong 'hobby' so that I had a keen interest in learning the newer concepts of 'public finance', 'global trade', 'international currency exchange' and hundreds of other subjects that I knew little, or nothing about. My instructor was a professor who was approximately half my age, and who apparently was extremely bright, and quite possibly was intellectually brilliant. He was obese and wore glasses that constantly slipped down his nose and he habitually pushed them back into place while he lectured or scribbled on the blackboard. He wore nondescript unlaundered dress shirts, without a tie, that were partially tucked into his trousers. His pants were sometimes denim and sometimes corduroy, but always were worn so low that they only partially covered his crotch. His hair was a tonsorial disaster, although I doubt that he had ever been in a barber's chair. But what I found to be objectionable was that on the most basic level, the man lacked any ability to communicate!

If he was asked how a return of the United States to the 'gold standard' would affect foreign trade balances, he would turn to the blackboard, scribble a 'calculus of variations'(emphasizing his final point by slapping down his piece of chalk) and announcing "There!". On one occasion, when I questioned what "There!" meant, he turned to the blackboard, erased it in exasperation, covered the entire blackboard with a new equation, and then turned to me and said, "No, that's correct! I hadn't made a mistake!" He was totally incapable of explaining any economic concept by speaking English!

Top executives at prestigious firms have told me that it was corporate practice to only hire applicants holding degrees from Ivy League schools. Yet, I've worked with men and women, holding advanced degrees (some from Ivy League schools), that I couldn't trust to negotiate a social contract or a political settlement. I've known educators, whose every utterance had the tone of a pronouncement, but who were incapable of rational discourse. And of course, we've all known a few doctors, lawyers or engineers, who couldn't calculate the amount of a 15% tip on a restaurant tab.

In 2003, The Pew Charitable Trusts funded a survey which was conducted among college students in public and private schools. The New York Times reported on January 20, 2006,

> "More than 50 percent of students at four-year schools and more than 75 percent at two-year colleges lacked the skills to perform complex literacy tasks...College students could not interpret a table about exercise and blood pressure, understand the arguments of newspaper editorials or compare credit card offers with different interest rates and annual fees...Almost 20 percent of students pursuing four-year degrees had only basic quantitative skills. For example, the students could not estimate if their car had enough gas to get to the service station. About 30 percent of two-year students had only basic math skills...Overall, the average literacy of college students is higher than that of adults across the nation. Study leaders said that was encouraging but not surprising."

I would never advocate that we cease technocratic studies, however I believe that we must recognize that what technology does best, at least to the present time, is identify trends, problems, or conditions. Technology can identify communities that are experiencing spectacular growth, but is deficient when asked how best to house or transport the low income workers who service the needs of the growing community. (The Post-Katrina difficulties of the City of New Orleans are stark testimony in support of this observation.) Technology can identify the exact location of enemy troops, and can enumerate the most efficient means of killing these troops, but it has not provided techniques for providing solace to the relatives and families of the deceased combatants or civilian casualties. Technology can identify the lowest cost labor markets, but it hasn't developed the means of instructing a family how to survive on less than a living wage.

Educators must go back to the basics, and begin again to produce 'learned' men and women who are capable of problem solving and crisis management, or this nation will experience one debilitating crisis after another, until there is no industrial or social structure remaining.

THEATRE

Movies have impacted my social behavior and attitude for as long as I can remember. I recall that at the conclusion of the filmed version of the play, "Cyrano de Bergerac," I was startled back into reality when the lights were turned on in the cinema. However throughout my life, it has been staged drama that has profoundly moved and enraptured me. While many of the finest movies ever made were adaptations of earlier stage productions, the transference of a stage production to the silver screen seldom produces an improved product, and has on occasion completely destroyed the 'heart and soul' of the author's work.

Buffalo NY didn't have an active and constant theater presence during the 1950's. Occasionally, a road company would present a dated play at the Erlanger Theater (I remember seeing a production of "Mister Roberts" there), but for the most part Buffalonians had to be content with summer stock presentations of musicals at Melody Fair (a theater-in-the-round) for live staged entertainment. I first saw "South Pacific", "Call Me Madam", "Kismet", "Pajama Game", "Carousel", "Camelot", all excellent productions, at Melody Fair. There were two Melody Fair productions that left me agape and awed.

The first was "West Side Story". I knew that this show had been a big hit on Broadway, was based on Shakespeare's "Romeo and Juliet", and contained two of my favorite songs, 'Maria' and 'Tonight'. I was a little put off by the comment of Jack Paar, who said on his nightly talk show that he "was disturbed to see hoodlums running around in ballet shoes". But, from the moment that the show opened, I couldn't catch my breath. Bernstein's score, the dances, the songs, the acting, and the romantic story were completely unexpected and entrancing.

A year or so later, Barb and I, and a couple from Jamestown NY, the Lou Wallaces, went to see "Porgy and Bess". Once again, all that I knew about this musical was that Porgy was a black man, and that the score included two of my favorite songs, George Gershwin's 'Summertime' and "I Got Plenty o' Nuttin'". As the show opened, my first surprise was that Porgy was a 'cripple'. Next, was the fact that the entire cast seemed to be' black'. And then, to my horror, I had come to see an opera! My disappointment quickly disappeared as I got caught up in the beautiful music, the outstanding voices, and the human drama of the story. We were sitting in the second row, and during the scene where 'Crown' rapes 'Bess', it made me uncomfortable not to be able to help her. In the final scene, when Porgy asks "Where's Bess?" and is told that she went with 'Sporting Life' to New York, he desperately cries out "Where's New York?" and is told "up this road, way past the gas station!", I'm sitting in the second row, totally distraught, my face wet with tears, as Porgy starts on his arduous trek to rescue his beloved Bess while singing, "Oh, Lawd, I'm On My Way".

Meanwhile, I'm finding my enjoyment in drama by reading the Circle Drama Critic Award winning plays in my favorite hardcover book. I'm awed, as is everyone else, by Arthur Miller's "Death of a Salesman", "All My Sons" and "The Crucible", but I'm most intrigued by the themes and the content of the dramas written by William Inge. In particular, I can't seem to get enough of the drama, "Picnic". To this day I can't understand how any writer can convey so much information about his characters, in three acts, and in a little more than two hours of dialogue. By the time of the final scene, when 'Madge" boards the bus to join 'Hal' in Chicago, the audience has been told everything there is to know about 'Hal', 'Madge' and her sister 'Millie'. The dashed hopes and dreams of 'Flo', Madge's mother and her neighbor 'Mrs Potts' are well known to us, as are the ambitions and values of Madge's fiancée Alan, and his upper-crust father. And I think we all share the hope for marital bliss for the schoolteacher, 'Rose-Mary' and her storekeeper groom, 'Howard', in their mid-life union. It's like we knew these people all of our life.

Buffalo's image as a 'cultural wasteland' began to diminish in the 1960's when the Studio Arena Theater began producing first-rate drama in Downtown Buffalo, and state of the art theatres were constructed in nearby Niagara-on-the Lake Ont. and in Lewiston NY. The Bernard Shaw Festival, at Niagara-on-the-Lake, featured a repertory company of Shavian players that produced two, or three world-class productions each summer. At the Studio Arena Theater, I saw George Gizzard play "Cyrano de Bergerac", Jack Gilford in "The Price", and excellent presentations of "Come Back Little Sheba" and "Jacque Brel is Alive and Well, and Living in Paris". Perhaps, in my mind, the best production that I attended at The Studio Arena was Ibsen's "A Doll's House", starring a young Betsy Palmer. It was the first time that I had seen this play, and until then, I had never read any of Ibsen's work, so of course I was stunned by Nora's final farewell speech to her husband, as well as by her rejection of the security and comfort provided by her family and home. Upon further reflection, I was amazed at the modernity and aptness of this drama, which was first published in Sweden in 1879.

During the late 1960's and 1970's, Buffalo's Canadian neighbor, Toronto emerged as a world-class city, and with this emergence came first run Broadway musicals. It became quite fashionable for Buffalonians to spend a weekend in Toronto shopping, dining and seeing a stage show. Barb and I saw excellent productions of "Phantom of the Opera" and the pre-Broadway preview of the revival of "Showboat" in Toronto theatres. One of my most enjoyable experiences was seeing the musical "Kismet" performed by the Toronto Opera Company, despite the most uncomfortable seating I've ever had in a theater.

My most memorable theatrical evening occurred in Boston. Once again I was on a business trip, being squired around town as the newest member of New England Life Insurance Company's sales team. We were scheduled to have dinner and then attend a pre-Broadway opening presentation of "Funny Girl", which was already being proclaimed 'the year's smash hit'. During soup, our host announced that he had been unable to get tickets for the Barbra Streisand musical, and that we were going to have to settle for a less publicized drama, which was also headed for Broadway, after it's Boston 'rehearsal run'. The substitute offering was the London cast, headed by Paul Schofield and Albert Dekker, performing in "A Man for All Seasons".

Once again I knew nothing about this play and didn't know what to expect. Then, as the drama unfolded, a hush settled over the audience as the Duke of Norfolk, Cardinal Worsley, and King Henry VIII couched, pleaded, and finally threatened in their attempts to gain approval of the King's divorce plans. And when Thomas More answered their arguments, and parried the threats with logic and graciousness, there was audible gasping in expression of agreement and relief, throughout the auditorium. The political and intellectual conflicts were stimulating and emotionally draining. Yet the performance maintained a quiet humorous quality, as it related Thomas More's love and affection for his wife and daughter, even as political pressures pushed him to his inevitable demise. The audience's standing ovation and applause at the conclusion of the final act was the most heartfelt that I've ever witnessed.

On another occasion, this time while attending a 'housing' conference in Washington DC, I attended a pre-Broadway performance of "The Heiress", starring Jane Alexander and Richard Kiley, at the Kennedy Center for Performing Arts.

This stage presentation was based on the movie, which starred Olivia DeHaviland, Montgomery Clift, and Ralph Richardson, which in turn had been based on the staged play, "Washington Square". I had loved the movie, but I was completely enthralled by the performances of Kiley and Alexander. It was one of the best stage presentations, of any kind, that I have seen, but it never reached Broadway, being cancelled after it's Kennedy Center run.

I've attended a few performances in New York City and the presentations there, whether drama, musical comedy, or opera were always top-notch entertainment. I've seen shows in school auditoriums, barn theaters, public parks, Las Vegas lounges, intimate supper clubs, theater in the round, Globe Theatre facsimiles, converted movie palaces, and buildings specifically constructed for live stage presentations, but no matter where it's presented, "the plays the thing..." and in my mind, nothing in the entertainment world can compare to a 'live' stage performance.

978-0-595-40858-0
0-595-40858-3

Made in the USA